Scandinavian Knitwear

COLOUR, TEXTURE AND TECHNIQUES

RITA TAYLOR

Scandinavian Knitwear

COLOUR, TEXTURE AND TECHNIQUES

RITA TAYLOR

THE CROWOOD PRESS

First published in 2020 by
The Crowood Press Ltd
Ramsbury, Marlborough
Wiltshire SN8 2HR

www.crowood.com

British Library Cataloguing-in-Publication Data
A catalogue record for this book is available from the British Library.

ISBN 978 1 78500 665 4

Typeset by Kelly-Anne Levey
Printed and bound in India by Parksons Graphics

CONTENTS

ACKNOWLEDGEMENTS

Thank you first of all to my lovely models, Natalie, Grace, David and Liho; they have displayed the garments beautifully, and thank you to Helen who took most of their photographs. Many thanks to the Norsk Folkemuseum, the Alta Museum in Norway and the Digital Museum of Scandinavia for the use of their images, and thank you to the Knitting and Crochet Guild of the United Kingdom for the photographs of items in their collection. Lots of thanks to Hilary and Sue who made several of the swatches for me, and many thanks to Elly Doyle for her technical editing of the patterns. And last, but not least, special thanks to my husband for all his valuable help and support.

ABBREVIATIONS

General Abbreviations

alt	alternate	**pm**	place marker
approx	approximately	**psso**	pass slipped stitch over
beg	beginning	**rem**	remain(ing)
CC	contrast colour	**rep**	repeat
cont	continue; continuing	**rev. st. st**	reverse stocking stitch
dec	decrease; decreasing	**rnd(s)**	round(s)
DK	double-knitting	**RS**	right side
dpn	double-pointed needle	**sl1**	slip next stitch
g. st	garter stitch	**ssk**	slip next 2 stitches knitwise, one at a time, from the left-hand needle to the right-hand needle. Slip these 2 slipped stitches purlwise back on to left-hand needle and then knit these 2 slipped stitches together through the back loops
inc	increase by 1 stitch by knitting into front and back of next stitch (kfb), unless a different increase is specified by the pattern; increasing		
k	knit	**st(s)**	stitch(es)
k2tog	knit 2 stitches together	**st. st**	stocking stitch
kfb	increase by 1 stitch by knitting into front and back of next stitch	**tog**	together
m1	make 1 stitch by picking up horizontal loop lying before next stitch and knitting into back of loop	**WS**	wrong side
		wyib	with yarn in back (yarn at back of work)
MC	main colour	**wyif**	with yarn in front (yarn at front of work)
p	purl	**yo**	yarn over needle (also referred to as 'yarn on needle' [yon] or 'yarn round needle' [yrn] or simply 'yarn over')
p2tog	purl 2 stitches together		
patt	pattern		

Glossary of cable and twist stitches

1/1 LC   slip next stitch to cable needle, place cable needle at front of work, k1 and then k1 from cable needle.

1/1 LPC   slip next stitch to cable needle, place cable needle at front of work, p1 and then k1 from cable needle.

1/1 RC   slip next stitch to cable needle, place cable needle at back of work, k1 and then k1 from cable needle.

1/1 RPC   slip next stitch to cable needle, place cable needle at back of work, k1 and then p1 from cable needle.

2/1 LPC   slip next 2 stitches to cable needle, place cable needle at front of work, p1 and then k2 from cable needle.

2/1 RPC   slip next stitch to cable needle, place cable needle at back of work, k2 and then p1 from cable needle.

2/2 LC   slip next 2 stitches to cable needle, place cable needle at front of work, k2 and then k2 from cable needle.

2/2 LPC   slip next 2 stitches to cable needle, place cable needle at front of work, p2 and then k2 from cable needle.

2/2 RC   slip next 2 stitches to cable needle, place cable needle at back of work, k2 and then k2 from cable needle.

2/2 RPC   slip next 2 stitches to cable needle, place cable needle at back of work, k2 and then p2 from cable needle.

tw2L   twist 2 stitches left: knit into the back of the second stitch on the left-hand needle, but do not remove this stitch from the left-hand needle; now, knit into the front of the first stitch on the left-hand needle; and, finally, slip both worked stitches off of the left-hand needle. (Note that this is nearly equivalent to working a 1/1 LC.)

tw2R   twist 2 stitches right: knit 2 stitches together (k2tog), but do not remove these stitches from the left-hand needle; now, knit into the front of the first stitch on the left-hand needle, and slip both worked stitches off of the left-hand needle. (Note that this is nearly equivalent to working a 1/1 RC.)

INTRODUCTION

A real tradition is not a relic of the past that is irretrievably gone; it is a living force that animates and informs the present.

Igor Stravinsky, *Poetics of Music* (Harvard University Press, 1947).

An atmospheric picture giving the 'feel' of Scandinavia.

Scandinavia comprises Norway, Sweden and Denmark, with its associated territory of the Faroe Islands. The three countries are joined together, not separated by any large expanse of water or huge range of mountains. This fact is relevant to the knitting history of this region, as it seems that many of the designs and techniques overlap, with a few distinctions specific to some areas. The climate of the three countries varies depending on how far from the Gulf Stream they each are; in the central areas, it can be humid, while the northern areas of Norway and Sweden can have temperatures as low as −30°C. One third of Norway lies to the north of the Arctic Circle. Denmark has a relatively mild climate because of its proximity to the sea, but the summers are never particularly warm. Hence, there is a need for warm clothing in these countries.

The striking colours of Kristiansand.

A Scandinavian pine forest, with its range of colours and textures.

And warm clothing often equates to the versatile craft of knitting, a tradition dating back between 300 and 400 years in these lands.

Knitting appears not to have been widespread in Scandinavia until the sixteenth century. It is suggested that it was brought to Norway, Sweden and Denmark via the Netherlands. The textured patterns of the 'nightshirts' particularly illustrate this theory (see Chapters 3 and 5 for further information about these nightshirts).

While some of the patterns presented in this book are based on such traditional Scandinavian designs, others are inspired by the simplicity and clean lines familiar to us from this part of the world. As these countries can be cold and dark during the long winters, the emphasis is on warmth and light in the home, so knitted throws and cosy cushions use white or cream wool and have simple textured patterns. Bear this philosophy in mind as you create your own designs, and you will have pieces that you will be happy to display for many years.

On the other hand, the garments traditionally knitted for outdoor wear are often bright and colourful; red, yellow, green and blue are popular on a white or black background. But, as you will see here, it can be interesting to interpret the patterns with different colours, using images of Scandinavia as inspiration.

While this book contains patterns for recognizable Scandinavian knitwear, to wear and to furnish the home, the patterns are not direct copies of existing items. The chapters give ideas for creating designs of your own, using both the featured charts and swatches and the calculations that you will make, based on measurements that you will take. This is intended as a catalyst to help you to develop your own ideas. One of the advantages of hand knitting is the freedom to create 'on the hoof' as other ideas occur to you. Feel free to adapt, embellish and alter these patterns to suit yourself. I have assumed that you already have a good knowledge of the craft and that you are ready to follow the example of the inventive and skilled knitters of the past and to see for yourself how satisfying it is to create a project that you have planned and designed from start to finish. I hope that this book will encourage you to practise, experiment, keep or discard, each time adding to your knowledge, just as the early knitters did. Heed the words of Igor Stravinsky, and do the same, by letting your combined knitting experiences inform what you knit in the present.

CHAPTER 1

GENERAL KNITTING HISTORY

While knitting now seems to us to have been practised for thousands of years, its actual origins are quite obscure, and it is probably a much younger craft than we would imagine. If it were an ancient craft, you would expect there to be corresponding myths and legends relating to the various gods and goddesses, as there are for the weavers and the spinners, but so far no one has come across any.

Early pieces of knitting were probably made for practical reasons; as they wore out, they would be discarded. They were made from perishable fibres, and there are only fragments of fabric left to study, not whole pieces, which also makes it difficult to discern exactly how the pieces were constructed. They were also only small items, such as hats, stockings, mittens and bags or purses; there were no jumpers or jackets until much later.

CONSTRUCTING FABRIC

The earliest pieces that can be authenticated were usually made for special occasions, especially those involving religious ceremony, and these are often fine examples of the craft. Because the early pieces that have been discovered are only fragments, it is difficult to say precisely, but they appear to have been made by using a different technique to that of knitting as it is practised today.

There are various ways in which the fabric could have been constructed from lengths of fibre, several of which are introduced in the following sections.

Sprang

The early pieces of fabric could have been made by using a looped technique called 'sprang' that involves a frame similar to that of a small weaving frame. When the threads have been prepared and positioned vertically on the frame, they are then looped sideways over each other in turn and held in place with a rod. The earliest pieces of sprang have been found in Scandinavia, preserved by peat bogs, and date from around 1200BC.

Small fabric pieces could also be made in a similar way to that in which children make long lengths of cord by using a wooden 'dolly' or cotton reel with four nails inserted into the top. The pieces would be made flat on a series of pegs attached to a piece of wood. The yarn was initially wound around each peg, the next strand was then laid above the resulting loop on each peg and then the loop was lifted over the new strand and off the peg. As a handheld tool, intended to be portable, the peg frame was obviously not very big, and the fabric pieces would be made in strips, which later had to be joined together. There were slightly larger peg frames that would fit on the lap, but these would still not have been wide enough to create an adult-sized garment.

Naalbinding

Another way to create fabric from lengths of yarn was to use a single threaded needle and short yarn lengths that are pulled completely through the next loop to be worked and not be left to form another loop as in sprang or knitting. This technique begins with the formation of a chain of stitches that are worked in a similar way to that of buttonhole stitch in embroidery. These stitches are then joined into a ring, and, for the next row, the yarn is worked into the top of each loop. There is only one loop on the needle at a time and so naalbinding will not unravel as knitting does. It probably more closely resembles crochet than knitting.

There is a single sock made by using this technique in the Jorvik museum in York. It was found beneath a tenth-century building in Coppergate, and, as no other items made in this way have been found in England, it may well have come from the foot of a Scandinavian visitor. Earlier socks made by using this technique have been found in Egypt and date from the fourth century, so it would seem that this was the method most commonly used at the time for creating fabric from strands of fibre. It appears to have been most widely practised to create small items such as hats, mittens and socks. It is a slow process, and it would not have been worthwhile to use it to make full-size garments. When the much quicker technique of knitting was 'discovered', naalbinding faded out of use.

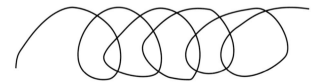

Naalbinding is constructed with short lengths of yarn that are threaded on to a needle to make a series of loops.

Knitting

Knitting as we know it, performed with two needles and a continuous length of yarn, may have begun somewhere in Africa and then been carried to Egypt by the Arabian desert tribes. Perhaps someone naalbinding tried not pulling the yarn all the way through the current stitch being worked but took the yarn through only halfway and left a loop, into which they made another loop? As more loops joined the chain, it might have become obvious that more rows of loops could be added above the first one, giving rise to the idea of working with a continuous length of yarn.

The earliest pieces identified as knitting involve colourwork. The Victoria and Albert Museum holds a fragment of a piece of knitting from Egypt: a sock dated to between 1000AD and 1400AD. It carries a small design of blue and white diamonds divided by bands of geometric shapes. Because of the intricacy of the construction, the shaping along the calf and of the heel and also the colourwork pattern, it is supposed that knitting must have been known and practised since much earlier than this time for the craft to have achieved such a high degree of complexity and for its practitioners to have acquired such a high degree of skill.

From Africa, knitting probably spread to Europe via the trade routes; it may have been its increased portability as opposed to the lack of portability of weaving, which requires cumbersome tools, that helped it to travel across the continents. While it was probably used to make basic necessities such as socks, mittens and undergarments, many more decorative pieces were made for religious purposes or for royalty.

A pair of complex pillow covers were found in the tomb of Prince Fernando de la Cerdo, who was buried in 1275AD, which gives these covers a reasonably accurate date of a little before this. The covers are decorated with birds and flowers, as well as various geometric shapes, and had been worked with purple, gold and white silk. Archaeological finds have reliably dated other knitted pieces to the fourteenth century. Again, they are patterned with several colours of silk.

As the technique of knitting spread, knitting guilds were established in parts of Europe, for example, in Paris in 1268 and in the Netherlands in 1469. The aim of these guilds was to encourage young men to become skilled masters of the craft. Knitting was primarily a male occupation; women treated and spun the fibres. After three years, an apprentice would attain the status of journeyman, able to knit hats, gloves, stockings and garments. For another three years, the journeymen were to travel the world, learning the techniques and practices of other cultures. So, it is easy to see how some motifs were spread from one area to another and why we cannot say that a particular motif has its origins in a specific country. When each of these young journeymen returned, he would work on his masterpiece, a carpet or wall hanging, featuring numerous depictions of flora and fauna, worked in many colours and measuring anything up to three metres long! Before he could become a master knitter, along with the various garments that he also had to knit, he was given thirteen weeks to complete this task.

As clothing styles and fashions developed, knitted garments became more in demand amongst the general populace. In the sixteenth century, doublet and hose (usually made from cloth) were replaced by knee breeches. These were worn with closely fitted stockings to show off shapely calves, and the flexibility of knitting made it more appropriate than woven fabric for this purpose. Similarly, it was easier to create gloves, with their separate fingers, by using a knitted fabric rather than piecing together cloth or leather. Many people, men and women, augmented their income by knitting such items, often for export. Of course, people knitted for themselves, making warm, practical garments to wear for working outdoors or as underwear and nightwear, sometimes by using lengths of wool that they had gradually saved from their outwork!

Almost all of these early items were knitted in the round. At some time during the sixteenth century, someone worked out how to create the ridges that appeared on the back of the fabric on the front, as a decorative feature. A pair of stockings with a round of such 'purl' stitches on the outside were found in the tomb of Eleanor of Toledo, who died in 1562. Purl stitches were frequently used as decoration subsequent to their discovery, showing how quickly techniques could travel, even in those times.

Very few everyday pieces of knitting from before the twentieth century have been preserved. The majority of knitted items would have been utilitarian items, made to be worn until they disintegrated. However, there are a few surviving items dating from the nineteenth and early twentieth centuries that show very high levels of craftsmanship, in particular exquisite lace shawls from the Faroe Islands, Shetland Islands, Orenburg

A set of cushions knitted with various Fair Isle motifs.

and Estonia, although, apart from the lace shawls of the Faroe Islands, there doesn't appear to be a tradition of knitted lace in Scandinavia.

Later came finely knitted colourwork pieces from Fair Isle and the Shetlands, the beautiful Bohus cardigans and sweaters from Sweden, and the ubiquitous pieces featuring the *Selburose* or Norwegian star. Most of the pieces that are preserved would have been special-occasion garments, gifts for weddings, or shawls and christening robes, kept to be passed on to the next generations.

A Shetland shawl with coloured edgings made in fine lace-weight yarn.

Reindeer are often depicted on Scandinavian costume in various guises.

The Norwegian star motif is particularly associated with Scandinavia but is actually an old motif found in many parts of the world.

SCANDINAVIAN KNITTING

The easiest items of all to knit were caps and mittens, and these were very popular in the colder northern climate.

Each country, and even each district of a country, had their own identifiable shapes and designs, and several places became so well known for a particular style that their work was exported to other parts of Europe. While Norway was one of the last places to adopt knitting, it is now firmly associated with the distinctive motif of the Norwegian star, found on many pairs of mittens, as well as on many other items of clothing.

As knitting became more popular, so its practitioners became more inventive, and, by the eighteenth century, it was practised by many for pleasure and not for necessity. However, in many of the rural areas of Scandinavia, it was still a means of adding to the family income. All members of the family would take part, with children often working any ribbing and their parents taking over the more complex sections of an item. Patterns became ever more intricate with lace, travelling stitches and colourwork being included. With the discovery of synthetic dyes in 1856, even more colours were introduced, as can be see within these chapters, and there are now some very beautiful and exciting designs from each of the Scandinavian countries.

Scandinavian wool

While items for royalty or for religious purposes were invariably made from silk, and probably imported, the garments and accessories made for everyday wear by the general populace were made from the wool of whichever sheep were kept in and local to that region. Wool is especially useful in the colder, and often wetter, climes of the northern latitudes. It can absorb up to 30 per cent of its own weight when wet, without that wetness passing through to the body; in fact, the wet fibres actually help to generate a bit of heat. The insulating properties of wool mean that it can keep the heat out when it is hot and in when it is cold, which is particularly useful in Scandinavia.

The sheep of Scandinavia are small and hardy. There are various breeds, some with origins of thousands of years ago. Amongst them are the Gotland, Roslag, Rya and Svardsjo of Sweden, the ancient Faroese of the Faroe Islands, and the Rygya and Spelsau of Norway. These latter sheep breeds have been around for at least three-thousand years; they have coats

Gotland sheep.

composed of two layers: the fine, downy undercoat and the outer coat of coarser, hairy wool. The old Spelsau sheep would naturally shed their wool in the summer, but today they are shorn. The fleece is long and dense and perfect for hand knitting. When knitting was primarily done for the family, the wool would be plucked from the sheep or collected from the heathland bushes upon which the wool had been snagged or rubbed off. However, later, when knitting became more

of a cottage industry, the sheep would be shorn, often twice a year. The women would spin the wool, and all members of the family would be involved in the knitting, which was mainly of stockings and mittens. The people also organized knitting parties, especially when they were very busy with items for export. The finished items would be taken to the markets in the large towns to be sold, and trade was brisk. However, with the decline of knee breeches and the advent of trousers, the stocking trade declined. Mittens continued to be popular, and later the multicoloured patterns of ski jumpers gave another boost to the Scandinavian knitwear industry.

To achieve the closest look and feel to that of a traditional Scandinavian sweater, choose a wool such as Shetland that will stick to itself, especially if you are making something in stranded colourwork and that is being knitted in the round with steeks.

Fabric of stranded colourwork, or with textured patterns knitted in a single colour, is warmer than that made by using a single, unstranded yarn. The double layer produced by using two different colours is obviously warmer, but fabric of textured stitches, where the yarn has been repeatedly moved to the back and to the front of the work, has air trapped between the stitches, also giving a bit more insulation, which is an important consideration in the colder, northern climates.

Steeks

Steeks are added where you need to cut through the stitches of the knitted fabric in order to make front openings, armholes or neck openings. A few extra stitches are added, usually about ten, and these are worked alternately in the colours that you are using in each particular row. When the work is finished, a cut is made between the columns of the middle two stitches of the steek (so, for example, between the columns of the fifth and sixth stitches of a ten-stitch steek). The two separated sides of the cut steek are then sewn down on the inside of the work, to stabilize the steek sides and secure their stitches.

Styles and types of garments in each area

Some patterns and styles are found throughout Scandinavia, while others are unique to a particular area. Norway is known for its *Lusekofte*, a type of sweater, with their lower body worked in a pattern of single stitches of contrasting colours that is known as lice stitch!

It is also the area of the ubiquitous star or rose pattern, as found on the mittens of Selbu and on the Fana cardigans. While this motif is seen as a typical Norwegian design, Norwegians didn't invent it. Stars have always been a popular motif in many parts of the world, but Norway used it on so many items that it was bound to become fashionable. The company Dale of Norway has familiarized the rest of the world to these patterns.

Sweden has the distinctive all-over pattern that is known as Bjarbo as well as the unique designs of the Bohus sweaters and cardigans. Its other recognized technique is that of twined knitting, also known as *tvåändsstickning* or *twandstickning*, which gives a thick but less flexible fabric than that of stranded knitting.

Denmark is especially known for its damask sweaters and jackets, with their patterns of stars worked in purl stitches on a knit background. Like most of the knitted garments of Scandinavia, these were knitted in the round in a very basic shape of rectangles, sometimes with purl stitches marking the position of the side 'seams', in a similar way to the fisherman's ganseys of the North Sea coasts. Perhaps the textured patterns of knit and purl stitches may also have derived from these garments, or perhaps they were inspired by the intricate Dutch petticoats, with their pictorial patterns of flora and fauna.

A distant view of a sweater inspired by the ubiquitous Norwegian star patterns.

Similar textured items were worn as nightshirts (*nattrojer*) throughout these often-cold northern lands, but most of the Danish ones held by museums were knitted with silk and so were probably imported and intended for royalty. Similar motifs to those of the nightshirts but worked in two colours, rather than with textured stitches, decorated the silk brocade jackets, dated to the early seventeenth century, that were found in the coffins of two children of King Christian IV of Denmark.

On the Faroe Islands, as well as the type of warm, comfortable clothing seen on the mainland, there was also a tradition of making and wearing fine knitted shawls. They are of an unusual construction in that they are made in three panels: a narrow central one and left and right wings. They also have short darts at the shoulders that help to keep the shawl in place when it is being worn. They are knitted in

The right side of a piece of twined knitting.

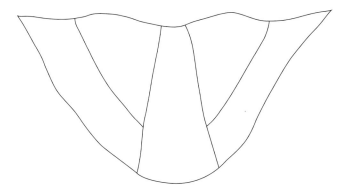

Diagram showing the unusual shape of a Faroese shawl. The central panel would often have a different lace pattern to that of the side wings.

garter stitch with assorted lace patterns and worked from the bottom edge upwards. The knitters use the finest wool from the undercoat of the local sheep and leave it undyed in shades of brown, grey and cream, just as it comes from the sheep.

For the general populace, the early garments were again made from wool just as it came from the sheep, undyed and in its natural colours, ranging from cream to dark brown. Later, subtle colours were introduced by using natural dyes derived from various plant materials; it was not until the mid-nineteenth century that chemical dyes were discovered and the range of colours being used became much brighter and bolder.

The patterns contained in this book are inspired by these traditional garments with their elaborate designs. The charts and swatches in Chapter 6 can be utilized in several different ways. For example, some of the two-colour motifs could be worked in a single colour as textured patterns, by instead using purl stitches in place of the second colour. Many of the designs used in Scandinavian knitting are derived from counted-thread embroidery, familiarly used on many of the national costumes, such as this piece taken from a book of cross-stitch motifs.

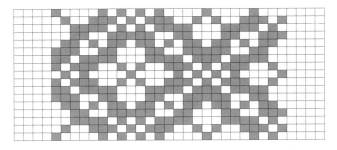

An embroidery chart featuring the ubiquitous star motif.

Books and patterns

Pattern books were first printed in Germany in the sixteenth century and were widely available. The designs were drawn out on squared paper; this is ideal for translating into knitting, as can be seen in the featured copy of a motif on a knitted pincushion.

Knitting-instruction books were also widely available from the nineteenth century, which also helped to popularize the craft; from this time onwards, knitting was found in all parts of the world in its various styles.

The first printed pattern leaflets for individual items appeared at the beginning of the twentieth century. As knitting became more popular, more yarn spinners and manufacturers introduced their own patterns, and, gradually, the uniqueness of some of the knitting traditions disappeared. It is difficult to tell now exactly where a pattern or motif originated, but the knitting of Scandinavia does seem to have a style all of its own.

A drawing of the design on a knitted pincushion held in the Victoria and Albert Museum, London.

Printed patterns became more readily available from the 1950s.

A pair of intricately worked mittens with a reindeer motif. Item NF.1899-0457/Norsk Folkemuseum.

A Scandinavian jumper with what might be described as a typical Icelandic yoke, showing how similar the styles of garments were between these two locations.

STARS JUMPER

This jumper is worked flat but could be worked in the round with steeks for the armholes or be divided to work the back and front parts of the yoke separately. Many Norwegian jumpers were worked in this way, but the sleeves were often knitted in the round from the cuff upwards and sewn into the armholes. Choose whichever method suits you best.

Size

To fit a chest circumference of 36in
Actual measurements: chest circumference 38in; back length 25in; sleeve-seam length 17½in

Materials

6 × 50g balls of aran-weight yarn in main colour (MC)
50g of aran-weight yarn in contrast-colour 1 (CC1)
50g of aran-weight yarn in contrast-colour 2 (CC2)

Needles

1 pair 3.75mm needles
1 pair 4mm needles
1 pair 5mm needles
Circular 4mm needle

Tension

16sts and 19 rows to 10cm/4in using 5mm needles over st. st

Back

Using 4mm needles and CC2, cast on 81sts, and work 2 rows of k1, p1 rib.
Change to CC1, and work k1, p1 rib until piece measures 2in from cast-on edge.
Change to 5mm needles and CC2. Knit across row, and, at the same time, dec by 1 stitch at end of row. (80sts)
Join in MC, and work border chart.
When border chart is completed, work 9in more of st. st with MC.
For yoke, beg by working lower-edge-of-yoke chart, and, at the same time, dec evenly to 73sts on last row.
Work 3 large stars across yoke by following large-stars chart, and, at the same time, inc evenly to 78sts on last row.
Next, work upper-yoke chart.
When work measures 25in from cast-on edge and upper-yoke chart is completed, leave all sts on a holder.

Detail of stars jumper.

Front

Work as for back to 10 rows fewer than were worked for back (that is, ending after row 10 of upper-yoke chart is completed).

Neck shaping
Patt 33sts, slip 12sts on to a holder for front neck, patt to end.
Dec by 1 stitch at neck edge of every row until 23sts remain.
Slip these 23sts on to a holder for right shoulder.
Return to rem 33sts, for left front, and work these sts as for right front.

Join each shoulder with a three-needle cast-off, using 23sts from relevant side of back and shoulder holder, leaving 32sts at centre of back for back neck.

Neckband

Using a 4mm circular needle and CC1, knit 32sts from back neck, pick up and knit 11sts down left-front neck edge, knit 12sts from front-neck holder and pick up and knit 11sts from right-front neck edge. Work 6 rounds of k1, p1 rib.
Change to CC2, and work 2 more rounds of rib as set.
Cast off loosely in patt.

Border

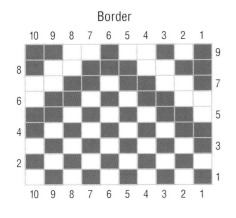

Upper yoke

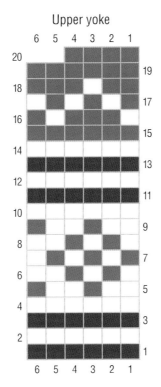

Lower edge of yoke

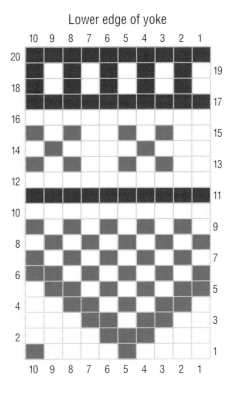

Key

☐ Main colour

RS: knit
WS: purl

☐ repeat 24 sts

■ CC1

■ CC2

Large stars

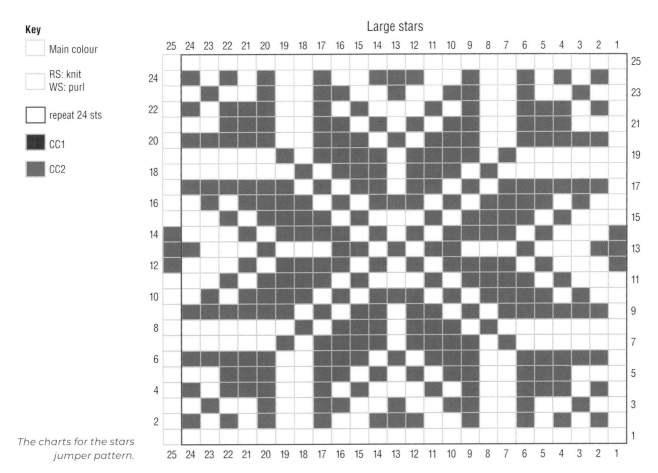

The charts for the stars jumper pattern.

OPPOSITE PAGE: *Detail of the pattern at the top of the sleeves.*

Sleeves

Using 5mm needles and CC1, pick up and knit 71sts around one armhole, starting and ending at beg of large-stars patt. Work sleeve chart, and, at the same time, dec at each end of every 6th row until 47sts rem. Note that the pattern will not always fit exactly into the number of available stitches.
Work even in st. st with MC until piece measures 15in from armhole edge.
Next row: Dec to 41sts as follows: (k5, k2tog) to last 5sts, k5.
Change to 3.75mm needles and CC1, and work 12 rows of k1, p1 rib.
Change to CC2, and work 1 row of k1, p1 rib.
Cast off loosely in patt.

Work second sleeve as for first sleeve.

Finishing

Sew both side seams and sleeve seams, and weave in all yarn ends.

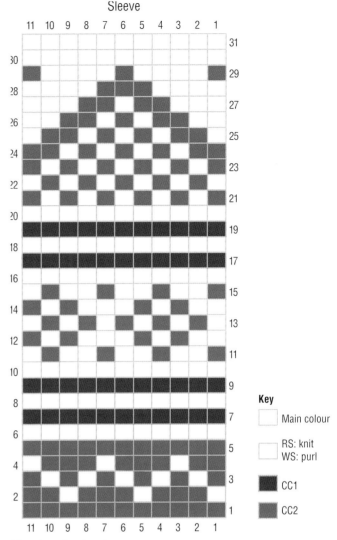

Sleeve

Key

☐ Main colour

☐ RS: knit
WS: purl

■ CC1

■ CC2

The chart for the sleeve.

If you wish to make this jumper in a different size, you will need to choose patterns that will fit into your required number of stitches.

For a 32in chest circumference with a couple of inches of ease, this will mean casting on 72sts; a 40in chest circumference will require about 90sts, a 44in chest about 100sts, and so on, with about 8sts more on the back and on the front for each additional 4in of the chest-circumference measurement.

If you wish to include the large stars then add filler stitches or a small filler motif between each one, or, for larger sizes, work four stars. They are worked over 24sts each, so four of them will fit nicely into 96sts and, with an edge stitch at each end, that would work for the 44in size.

The triangular border and lower-edge-of-yoke patterns can be easily adjusted to fit the required number of stitches, and the smaller patterns can be spaced differently.

CHAPTER 2

TECHNIQUES AND TIPS

FINDING INSPIRATION

Inspiration comes from many places; sometimes an idea will just come seemingly unannounced into your head, but, usually, it is the sight of something – a beautiful view, another person's sweater, a group of colours – that will trigger an idea for your piece of knitting.

Most of my inspiration comes from outdoors. There is so much variety in nature; shapes, texture and colour can all provide ideas for cables, textured patterns and colourwork.

Trees, and especially their bark characteristics, are also useful inspiration for cable patterns.

Brizlee Tower in Hulne Park, Northumberland, with its interesting shapes and motifs.

The aurora borealis provides an idea for a colour scheme.

A picture of Trondheim that suggests another interesting colour scheme.

The lovely textured bark of a beech tree.

Other crafts are also a source of design inspiration. Many an embroidery motif has been translated into a knitting pattern. It was quite possibly the source for the ubiquitous Norwegian star motif, as seen on the featured drawing of a pincushion motif.

Buildings, and their shapes and patterns, inside and out, are another useful source, as are floor and wall tiles, gates and fences.

Make lots of sketches of anything interesting that you see around you, and keep a note of colours and shapes that inspire you.

Tree trunks can be used as inspiration for colours or textures.

A close-up of the yoke of the Norwegian stars sweater.

A diamond-patterned window pane that can be used as inspiration for travelling-stitch or cable patterns.

conform to the shape of the body wearing it. Put your ideas on paper by making a sketch, then add notes about yarn, colour and variations that you might make.

When you have all of your ideas down on paper, take a full set of body measurements.

PLANNING YOUR DESIGN

There may be different styles and construction methods associated with various areas of Scandinavia, but, when you are creating a design, whatever the origins, the same tenets apply to all of them: spend time on planning and preparation. Decide on the shape that you would like to achieve; consider whether that shape flatters you (or the recipient); try on some of your existing garments and choose the shape, sleeve style and neckline that you feel happiest with.

The simplest shaped garment for the upper body, and the one that was most often constructed before the advent of complex patterns derived from the shapes of tailored garments, is composed of four rectangles. The elasticity of knitting helps the garment, despite its box-like shape, to

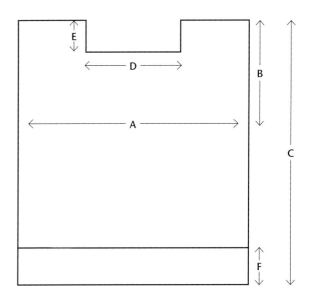

A sketch of a basic box-shaped sweater, with marked positions of important measuring points. A = width of chest; B = depth of armhole; C = full length; D = width of neck; E = depth of neck; F = depth of hem/welt.

A man sizing up a tree while wearing a Lusekofte-inspired sweater.

Measuring

It is best to have someone to help you with measuring, as some of these measurements can be quite awkward to take on your own. If you have a garment that fits you well and you like the style and shape of it, you can measure that instead.

Chest circumference
Measure around the fullest part of your chest, ensuring that the tape measure is parallel to the floor. The back and front of your garment will be one half of this circumference measurement plus however much you decide to add on for comfort and ease.

Torso level
This is the point on the body where any armhole shaping would end on the garment, about midway between the shoulder and the chest. The torso level can be described as a distance measured up from the waistline or from the level of the fullest part of the chest or down from the top of the shoulder.

Neck circumference
Measure around the largest part of the neck. If you are creating a circular neckline and would like to make a wider neck, you can add inches here. However, I would not recommend making the neckline circumference more than 25cm/10in larger than your actual neck circumference.

Neck depth

For a round or V-neck shape, measure where the shaping is to start below the lowest part of the neck. This point should be no less than 6cm/2½in for a crew neck, although it can be less than this for a wide, shallow neckline.

Armhole depth

Measure from the top, outside edge of the shoulder down to the armpit in a perpendicular line.

Body length

Measure from the underarm to your desired garment length.

Waist circumference

Measure around the narrowest part of your body. If you are not sure exactly where this is, tip from side; your natural waist will be at the tipping point.

Back-to-waist length

Measure from the most prominent bone at the base of the neck to the natural waist.

Hip circumference

Measure around the widest part of the hips (often about 17–18cm/6¾–7in down from the natural waist). Turn slightly sideways in front of a mirror while taking this measurement, so that you can see whether the tape measure is positioned at the fullest part of your body.

Waist-to-hips length

Measure from your natural waist to where you placed the tape measure around your hips for the hip-circumference measurement.

Sleeve length

Measure from the armpit to where the cuff should end, with the arm slightly bent and the tape measure following the bent line of the arm.

Upper-arm circumference

Measure around the widest part of the upper arm, the bicep.

Wrist circumference

Measure around the wrist where the hand joins the arm.

Head circumference

For a hat, measure around the head, with the tape measure running across the forehead and over the ears.

Head depth

Again for a hat, measure the depth from the head-circumference line to the top of the head.

Mark these measurements on your sketch. Make a photocopy of it (or many, if you are planning to knit more garments) so that you can also use it to mark the positions of the various stitch motifs that you might like to incorporate. Keep a note of these measurements, and those of anyone else that you are knitting for. You will probably want to add a few extra centimetres for ease (discussed in more detail in the following section), depending on how fitted you want the garment to be; 5–10cm/2–4in is the usual amount.

If you are knitting for someone whose measurements you don't know then there are tables of measurements available for the average person; these tables can be found in many knitting-technique books.

Once you have all of the necessary measurements, it is time to decide how much allowance needs to be added into the garment in order for it to feel comfortable when worn.

Ease

Using the diagram of your chosen sweater shape and the actual body measurements noted, decide how much ease you would like for the style of the piece. The appropriate ease for a garment may be negative ease, zero ease or positive ease. Negative ease for part of a garment means that the garment will actually measure less than your corresponding body measurement. For a sweater, this means that it will have that form-fitting shape so familiar from 1930s and 1940s sweaters. The circumference of a zero-ease sweater will be that of your actual chest circumference or less, and this degree

The colourful yoke of the Bohus cardigan.

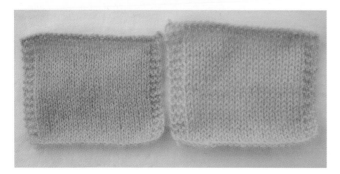

A swatch of worsted-spun wool yarn on the left and one of woollen-spun wool yarn, with its fluffier look, on the right.

The different shades of the fleece of Gotland sheep.

of ease is best suited to the typical hourglass shape that we women all aspire to! Positive ease is usually about five centimetres or two inches more than the chest-circumference measurement but can be even more when the fashion is for loose, oversized garments.

Most Scandinavian knitwear has been and is made with some positive ease, as it is intended to be worn over other garments.

YARN

Next, choose your yarn. For textured work, such as the damask-type knitting of Denmark, a smooth wool works best, as it gives good stitch definition, with strong contrast between the motifs.

The landrace sheep of Scandinavia, similar to Shetland sheep, provide the ideal wool for stranded colourwork knitting. This wool takes dye well but also comes in a wide range of natural colours. The Gotland sheep has a varying coat of silvery grey to almost black.

These were the wools that were traditionally used, just as they came from the sheep and being spun locally by the women. Colours varied from cream to dark brown, but some subtle colours were made by using natural dyes. It was not until the nineteenth century that chemical dyes were discovered, which allowed the motifs to be made much brighter and bolder. For a traditional look, use reds, blues, greens and yellows on a black or cream background; if you want to be more adventurous, try subtle pinks, mauves, turquoises and mustards instead. The variegated and self-striping yarns can be too distracting in colourwork, but muted heathery hues can work well, and I have used an ombré-type yarn for the Lusekofte-inspired sweater. But, for best results, clear, evenly dyed, strong colours of a smoothly spun wool allow the motifs to show up best.

An exception to this is yarn to be used for the Bohus-knitting technique of Sweden, where the colours are intended to meld together. The garments produced with this technique were made from a finer-weight, wool-blend yarn, with contrast stitches in angora yarn, often being worked as purl stitches, giving a soft, hazy look to the colourwork.

For a textured garment, choose a worsted-spun wool. This is prepared from longer fibres that are combed so that they all lie in the same direction. When spun, a smooth, dense yarn is made, ideally suited to seeded or damask-type patterns.

Woollen-spun yarns are made from shorter fibres that are carded, making them lie in various directions. When spun, a lighter and slightly fluffy looking yarn is produced, ideal for colourwork.

The more loosely spun woollen-spun yarns also grip one another better than do tightly spun yarns, helping to close up any gaps where the changeovers of colours occur.

This property of wool, to stick to itself, makes wool the best fibre to use for garments to be knitted in the round with steeks that will later be cut through to form armholes or front openings. When working with wool yarns, you can happily cut between a line of stitches without fear of the knitted fabric unravelling. Incidentally, no one seems to know where or how the term steek originated.

Tip

When you have selected your yarn, choose your buttons next. It is often more difficult to find buttons of the right size and colour to compliment your yarn and garment than it is to make your buttonholes of the correct size when you already have the buttons.

A beautifully knitted, multicoloured sweater from Norway. Item NF 2013-0563 Haakon Harriss/Norsk Folkemuseum.

Wraps per inch

If you have spun your own yarn, or have a yarn with no label, wrapping it around a ruler, or piece of dowelling, will give you an idea of what size of needles to first try working the yarn with. If you are using dowelling, cut a notch in one end and then make marks along it at one-inch intervals. Tape the end of the yarn to the ruler, or catch it into the notch in the dowelling. Gradually twist the ruler or dowelling so that the yarn winds around it, butting each strand up to the one before it. Wrap the yarn over 2in or 3in of the body of the ruler or dowelling, and then count how many strands there are. Take an average by dividing this number by however many inches over which you wrapped the yarn. Fourteen wraps per inch would equate to a double-knitting-weight yarn, so your first swatch would be made with 4mm needles; twelve wraps per inch is nearer to being an aran-weight yarn, and 5mm needles would therefore be an appropriate size to choose to work your swatch with.

Norwegian and Faroe Islands styles together.

COLOUR THEORY

Many items of Scandinavian knitwear are bright and colourful; the technique of working with two colours at once results in a garment that is warmer than one knitted with a single strand of yarn throughout. Most motifs are worked with two colours per row, but some of the traditional garments had highlights of a third colour, especially those of the Bohus designs. For the most part, the patterns included here use only two colours per row.

A colour wheel is a useful design tool for knitters. They are available to purchase, or you can make one of your own. Featured here is one that I made, but they are usually available in shops selling art materials.

The three main colours – red, yellow and blue – are equidistant from one another and are called 'primary colours'. They are separated by what are called the 'secondary colours'; a mix of one primary colour with its neighbouring one.

The secondary colours are separated further by the 'tertiary colours'; a mix of the primary colour with one of its neighbouring secondary colours.

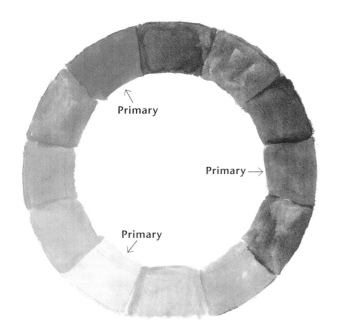

A colour wheel showing the primary colours.

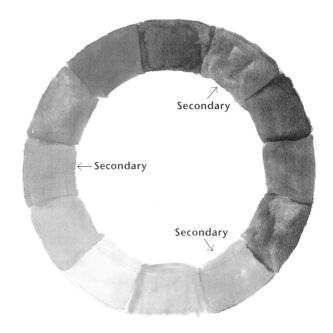

The colour wheel showing the secondary colours.

Many Scandinavian designs have an expanse of a neutral or main (background) colour too, so bear this in mind when choosing your contrast colours. Decide whether you want your piece to have a cool or a warm feel. Cool is anything from the blue side of the wheel; warm is anything from the red side. Next, decide whether to use a strong contrast, by choosing colours from opposite sides of the wheel, such as red and yellow, or yellow and blue, or whether you want a more subtle change of colour, by pairing a primary colour with a secondary or tertiary one. The colours – rusty red paired with a greenish blue – used for the featured flower-pattern mittens and headband are an example of this selection.

If you are not sure whether this more subtle colour scheme will work, photograph your swatch, and then print it in black and white. If the pattern disappears, the contrast of the colours is not strong enough, so you will have to try again with either a lighter or darker shade of one of the colours or a different colour altogether.

Working with three or more colours gets even more exciting. Picking three colours that are evenly spaced around the wheel produces what is known as a 'triadic' colour scheme. It is best used with one colour being dominant, with the other two as accents, as seen in the featured swatch for the border pattern, where red is used sparingly.

For four or more colours, the most pleasing results are achieved by using pairs of complementary colours, those

This headband and matching mittens are featured in Chapter 3.

A sample of Binge knitting.

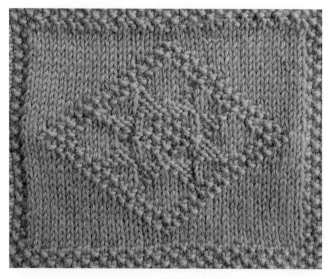

A swatch of a textured enclosed-star motif.

WORKING STRANDED COLOURWORK

Working with two colours at once

For the most part, only two colours are held at one time when working stranded colourwork, although some Scandinavian patterns do involve three, or even more, colours at once; this is especially so in the case of Bohus patterns.

There are various ways of holding the yarns when working with two colours; commonly, this is with the main-colour yarn on the index finger and the contrast-colour yarn on the middle finger or both yarns, one yarn held below the other, on the index finger of the left hand, or with one colour being held in the right hand and the other in the left hand. It takes quite a bit of practice to master these techniques, and the work will seem quite awkward at first, but the more you work at it the more 'normal' it will become for you.

Holding the yarn
The most popular way of holding the yarns seems to be to hold one strand with the right hand and one with the left. This is also the easiest way to catch in long floats, where there is a large number of stitches between the changes of colour, as there often are in Scandinavian designs. Always keep each of the yarn strands of the two colours in the same position on the hand or hands throughout the working of a item; when the strands are being worked with, the main-colour (background-colour) strand should stay below the strand of the contrast colour, so that the contrast-colour strand creating the motif will be lifted above the background-colour strand and therefore stand out more.

If none of these methods work for you then each yarn colour can be dropped, when it is no longer needed to work the next stitch, in order for the next yarn colour to be picked up, but this method is slower and can lead to uneven tension.

Working with several colours at once
Some Scandinavian patterns require more than two colours in a row. An example of this is found in Bohus knitting, where a third, contrasting colour is introduced to form purl stitches on the right side of the fabric.

from opposite sides of the colour wheel. But, sometimes, the best way to select your colours is to throw all of your balls of yarn on to the floor and to pick out those that look best next to each other!

If you are knitting a single-colour, textured garment, choose a solid, evenly dyed wool to show off the pattern best and not one that is too dark, otherwise the more elaborate motifs won't show up.

There is a tool known as a Norwegian ring, or knitting thimble, that is slipped on to the finger of either the right or left hand, depending on how you prefer to carry your contrast-colour yarns. There are different designs available: one has a row of pins with a cap over it; another has rings at the top and bottom, through which the yarns are threaded, with one colour in each ring. The third-colour yarn is carried in the other hand. Alternatively, both of the contrast-colour yarns can be carried on the finger and thumb of one hand – thus keeping them separate – to be plucked, as in continental knitting, by dipping the thumb out of the way when using the finger. The main-colour yarn is again held with the other hand.

As you knit, spread the stitches out across the right-hand needle, so that the work does not become pulled in and puckered. Before you start your intended item, knit some practice pieces, alternating the colours, until you become adept at keeping an even tension. Work other swatches with motifs of five or more stitches to practise carrying floats or catching them in. To catch in a long float, lift the non-working

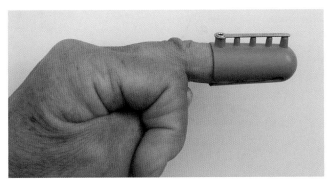

An example of a Norwegian knitting thimble.

Swiss darning

When you are working a third colour of yarn as knit stitches on a knit background and it is only for small spots of colour, it is often quicker to Swiss darn this colour. First, work the pattern by using only the first two colours of yarn, as specified by the chart. After completing the patterned fabric, thread the third-colour yarn through a tapestry needle, and, following the lines of the already knitted stitches and route of the yarn that forms these underlying stitches, work over the relevant stitches with the third-colour yarn, again by following the chart.

yarn on to the left-hand needle, place the working yarn – the one that is of the colour for the next stitch – on the same needle and then drop the non-working yarn before knitting the next stitch with the working yarn.

Colourwork is best worked in the round, as it is easier to see how the pattern develops, but also a better tension is kept when the work is not turned at the end of each row.

STEEKS

Garments were originally knitted as practical clothing, for keeping out the cold and wet; they were not made so that the wearer would be fashionable. Fashion came later with the advent of patterns from the various yarn companies, who introduced different shapes of what was essentially the same garment, with a V-neck or a round neck, or set-in sleeves or raglan sleeves, and so on. The knitters of old worked entirely in the round, sometimes with extra stitches, now known as a steek, added where any gaps were required.

For example, if you wish to make a cardigan entirely in the round, add about eight extra stitches at the centre front as a steek. Work these steek stitches in the colours that you are using for a particular round, arranging them alternately, and, to make it easier to find the centre, place an extra piece of yarn as a marker in the centre of the steek (either in the centre stitch for a steek with an odd number of stitches or between the two stitches at the centre of a steek with an even number of stitches). When the work is finished, either machine stitch or work back stitch by hand sewing along one stitch column on each side of the steek's centre. Cut along the centre column of stitches or between the two stitches at the centre of the steek, and fold the resulting steek edges to the inside of the garment. Either hem the steek edges in place, or work a row of crochet stitches along them and then stitch them in place, without distorting the fabric, to secure the steek stitches and prevent the steek edges from folding out and showing on the right side of the garment. For a cardigan, for example, next, pick up the stitches for the front band along the fold, and work the band in the usual way.

Steeks can also be used at the front neck. For a V-neck sweater, mark the centre-front stitch, work across the first set of stitches, then decrease by working k2tog, k1 before the marker. Cast on 8 stitches with alternate colours for the steek, k1, ssk and work to the end of the round. Now, work the shaping as described in the pattern, and keep working those

8 steek stitches at the centre front. When the work is finished, cut through the centre of the steek, fold the steek edges back, and hem them in place, before working the neckband along the fold of the steek, as for a cardigan. For a round neck, slip the centre stitches on to a holder, or on to waste yarn, as this is more flexible, then work as for the V-neck, creating the shaping as described in the pattern.

Armholes, where they are curved for joining to set-in sleeves, can be made in the same way as a round neckline, but traditional knitted garments were usually made with straight armholes, and these are worked in the same way as the centre front of a cardigan.

If you are using wool with the same characteristics as Shetland wool, this will eventually felt into itself and stick together, so there is no need to hem the steek edges in place, to secure the steek stitches and ensure that the steek edges remain on the inside of the garment, but other types of wool will probably need hem stitching.

Steeks can be used on plain-knitted or cabled garments too, and, in this case, it is probably a good idea to work the central two stitches of the steek in a contrasting colour, making it easy to see where the cutting line should be.

GRAFTING

Now often referred to as Kitchener stitch, grafting is a way of joining two sets of stitches together seamlessly. The instructions provided are for when you are working in stocking stitch and in rib stitch.

Grafting stocking stitch

Because the word 'needle' is used to describe two different tools – the knitting needle and the tapestry needle – it might seem ambiguous to refer to them both as 'needles' in this description. Therefore, I will refer to the knitting needle as a 'pin', which is the term that was frequently used to refer to knitting needles in previous times (they had a head and so were classed as pins, rather than needles).

To prepare for grafting, lay the two pieces to be grafted with the wrong sides facing each other and the points of both knitting pins that are holding the live stitches heading to the right.

Thread a tapestry needle with a length of yarn about three times the width of the piece to be grafted.

1. Bring the threaded tapestry needle forwards through the first stitch on the front pin as if to purl, and leave the stitch on the pin.
2. Take the needle through the first stitch on the back pin as if to knit, and leave the stitch on the pin.
3. Bring the needle through the first stitch on the front pin as if to knit, and slide the stitch off of the pin.
4. Bring the tapestry needle through the next stitch (now closest to the point of the pin) on the front pin as if to purl, and leave it on the pin.
5. Take the needle through the first stitch on the back pin as if to purl, and slip it off of the pin.
6. Take the needle through the next stitch (now closest to the point of the pin) on the back pin as if to knit, and leave it on the pin.
7. Repeat the last four steps (steps 3–6) until all the stitches have been worked off of the pins.

Grafting ribbing

This is done in two main stages.

1. Slip all of the knit stitches on to one pin and all of the purl stitches on to a second pin.
2. Arrange the two pins so that the knit stitches are on the front pin and the purl stitches are on the back pin, and then work as described for grafting stocking stitch.

BUTTONHOLES

Horizontal buttonholes

The neatest buttonholes are worked over one row, in the following steps:

1. Work to the intended position of your first buttonhole, take the yarn to the front of the work, and slip 1 stitch purlwise from the left-hand needle to the right-hand needle. Next, take the yarn that is at the front of the work to the back of the work.
2. Slip 1 stitch purlwise from the left-hand needle to the right-hand needle.
3. Pass the second stitch on the right-hand needle over the

first stitch on the right-hand needle as if to cast off.

4. Repeat the last two steps (steps 2–3) as many times as there are stitches that you need to cast off.

5. Slip the last stitch on the right-hand needle back to the left-hand needle.

6. Turn the work, and cast on the same number of stitches as were cast off plus 1 stitch to the left-hand needle.

7. Slip the first stitch on the left-hand needle to the right-hand needle.

8. Pass the just-slipped extra cast-on stitch over the previously slipped stitch on the right-hand needle (that is, the second stitch on the right-hand needle that was slipped in step 5).

9. Turn the work, and work to the position of the next buttonhole or as otherwise directed by the pattern.

Vertical buttonholes

These are usually worked on a band that is knitted vertically, either worked all in one with the garment or worked separately and sewn on, rather than on a horizontal band, where the stitches are picked up from the fabric edge and worked for the required number of rows.

1. Cast on the necessary number of stitches for the intended width of the buttonhole band (either as part of the main-garment cast-on or separately, for a sewn-on buttonhole band), then work across all of the buttonhole-band stitches for the necessary number of rows to reach the intended position of your first buttonhole.

2. To make the buttonhole, work across the first half of the stitches of the band for the necessary number of rows that will accommodate the diameter of the selected button.

3. Break the yarn, leaving an end of 3–4in.

4. Rejoin the yarn to the rest of the stitches of the band (the second half of the stitches of the band), and work the same number of rows as were worked for the first half of the stitches.

5. Next, work across both sets of stitches (that is, again across all of the stitches of the band), and continue working the band until reaching the intended position of the next buttonhole.

6. Use the resulting yarn ends that are adjacent to each buttonhole to reinforce the edges of the buttonholes.

CHARTS

The patterns for colourwork knitting are usually presented as charts. These charts can appear confusing at first, but, once you understand how they work, they are more readily understandable than line-by-line instructions. In the past, most knitters would create their own charts by simply making dots on the page of an exercise book, or they would fill in the squares of graph paper. We are lucky now in that there are a number of programs for creating charts on the computer, which can save time.

It is easy to see from a chart what the motif will look like when it is completed. This is very useful if you are designing a garment yourself. Unlike for written instructions, it is also easier to see how many stitches each motif will take up. The charts shown in Chapter 6 could all be worked by following the chart and not by using any written instructions.

Following a chart

A typical chart – and certainly the charts included in this book – is made up of a block of squares with numbers along the bottom and side(s). Each of the squares represents one stitch, and the number at the bottom of the chart in line with each stitch tells you which stitch it is. Some of the charts here have a box drawn around a section of the squares; this represents

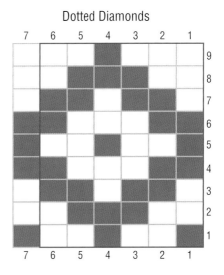

Dotted Diamonds

A chart for a Binge design, demonstrating how easy it is to visualize the pattern.

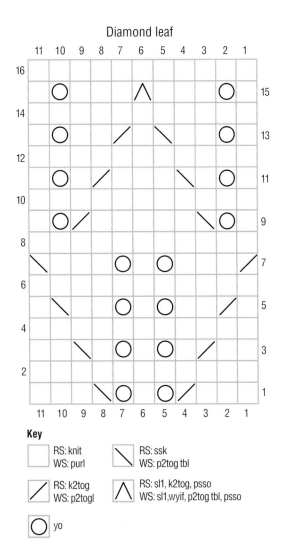

Diamond leaf

Key

RS: knit / WS: purl	
RS: ssk / WS: p2tog tbl	
RS: k2tog / WS: p2togl	
RS: sl1, k2tog, psso / WS: sl1,wyif, p2tog tbl, psso	
yo	

A chart with an accompanying key of the symbols used, to describe how to work the corresponding stitches.

the group of stitches that are repeated across the row and in line-by-line instructions would be indicated by an asterisk or brackets. The stitches outside of the box are worked only once, usually at the beginning or end of the row. When you reach the last row of the chart, to repeat the full motif represented by the chart, begin again from row 1 or from the first row within the pattern-repeat box, if present.

As an example, if you are knitting in the round, start at the bottom of the chart and work from right to left: the square designated by number 1 at the bottom of the chart and number 1 at the right side of the chart corresponds to the first stitch. It is coloured blue, which means that the stitch will be worked in the contrast colour; the next two stitches are left blank, which tells you that they will be worked in the main

(background) colour. Continue working the stitches with the relevant colours as indicated on the chart, repeating the section outlined in red, until you come to the end of the row; work the stitch outside the box.

Move up to the next row of squares (in line with number 2 at the right side of the chart), and work the stitches by following the colours for that row. Remember to read the chart row from left to right if you are not working in the round, so you will start with the single stitch outside of the red repeat box.

If this motif were given as written instructions for working back and forth, rather than for working in the round, the first two rows would read:

Row 1: *K1 C (where 'C' is 'contrast colour'), k2 MC (where 'MC' is 'main colour'); rep from * to last stitch, K1 C.
Row 2: P1 MC, *p1 MC, p3 C, p2 MC; rep from * to end.

As you can see, this is a cumbersome way of describing the pattern, and seeing it in pictorial form is much easier.

> **Tip**
>
> As you work through the chart, place a marker of some kind – a clear ruler is ideal – above or below the row that you are currently working.

For knitting in the round, you always read the chart from right to left, which makes it much easier to follow and easier to see how the pattern is developing.

Charts for textured patterns are usually made up of a series of dots that represent the purl stitches, although some older patterns might use crosses in the same way. Charts for Faroese lace shawls will contain symbols to indicate the formation of the eyelets, usually drawn as 'O'.

Do always read the key alongside the chart before starting to work from it. It might also include symbols for crossing stitches, increasing, decreasing and places where there is not a stitch. The latter is especially common in charts for rounded yokes.

SWATCHING

You have chosen your yarn, selected your motifs and picked out your colours. The next step is to work a swatch. This might seem time-consuming and unnecessary, but it will be a great help to see whether you really like your chosen colours together and are pleased with the drape and feel of the fabric, and it will also tell you whether the measurements you have taken will be met by the fabric to be worked with the yarn and needles being used. Treat and block the swatch in the way that you intend to treat and block your piece when you have finished it, and then measure the swatch to work out your tension.

Lay the piece of swatch fabric on a flat surface, and measure across the width of the fabric (excluding any border stitches) with a firm ruler; do not use a tape measure, as the material of the tape measure can stretch over time and lead you to take a false measurement. With pins, mark the stitch that is just after the zero mark of the ruler and the stitch just before the ten-centimetre (or four-inch) mark, then count the stitches between these pins. This will give you the number of stitches per ten centimetres (or four inches). Divide this number by ten to give you the number of stitches per centimetre (or by four to give you the number of stitches per inch). Follow the same method for the depth of the fabric, by marking and counting the vertical rows, to give you the number of rows per centimetre (or inch).

TOOLS AND EQUIPMENT

Needles

Knitting needles come in a wide variety these days and can be made from all kinds of materials. The earliest needles would have been made from wood or bone, but some have been found that were made from copper, dating from the Middle Ages. These needles would all have been double pointed, slightly tapered at both ends, as all knitting was done in the round. They can be seen in use in several paintings from the fourteenth century and also in those paintings mentioned in Chapter 5. These days, circular needles, first patented in America in 1918, are more likely to be used, with the two points either being fixed permanently to their cable or being interchangeable, with ends that click or screw into the cable

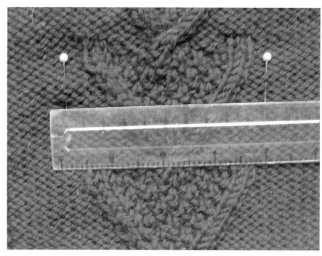

Measuring accurately to make sure that the tension is appropriate.

section. Knitting by using circular needles can be easier than knitting by using double-pointed needles (commonly referred to simply as 'dpns'), as the knitting is more evenly distributed and the section of fabric on the cable can lie in the knitter's lap. However, circular needles can be awkward to use when working narrow sections of a garment, such as the wrist part of a sleeve or a sock, and many people find that double-pointed needles suit them better here, while others prefer a long circular needle and a technique referred to as 'magic loop'. With magic loop, the stitches not being worked are pushed on to the cable and held at the back of the work while the needle points are operated to work the stitches nearer the knitter, just as though they were working with two needles. The best needles for working stranded or colourwork patterns have slightly rounded points that won't catch and split the yarn as easily as do long tapered points.

Before the publication of printed patterns, which invariably gave instructions for knitting the pieces in sections, almost all items were knitted in the round. In order to incorporate

Which needles to use?

When swatching, use the same needles that you think you will be using for the actual piece; you will be using circular needles for your piece if you will be knitting in the round, so knit your swatch in the round too. You can cut the resulting tubular swatch vertically from bottom to top, if you want to measure the fabric more accurately as a flat piece.

the shaping that was then fashionable, patterns were written that directed the knitter to construct the garment as being made from the shapes of sewn garments. This meant that separate pieces were knitted on two needles, back and forth, alternately working on the right and wrong sides of the fabric. These separate pieces then had to be joined together, so it was essential that the parts all matched each other, meaning lots of counting and measuring. This is not necessary when knitting in the round; the item is finished as soon as you put down your needles after working the last stitches of the garment!

Knitting in the round is quicker than knitting back and forth and then sewing the pieces together; this is an important consideration when the work was done for economic reasons. Before the fashion for garments made them more complicated, by introducing shaping at sides, armholes and necklines, almost everything was knitted as a tube, often with armholes or front openings that were cut when the work was finished. An advantage of this approach is that the face of the fabric is always available to the knitter, which makes it easier to follow the placement of stitches for textured and colourwork knitting.

Before the development of circular needles at the beginning of the twentieth century, those garments knitted in the round were worked on sets of double-pointed needles. A set of five, with two needles being worked with at a time, while the other three were left loose or held in a belt or sheath of some kind, was the most common. Dividing the work into four sections rather than three, as you do when using a set of four needles, made it easier to see the pattern placement in respect to its position on the body and also reduced some of the pull on the stitches positioned on the neighbouring needles.

Needle sizes

Current knitting needles are given a size based on their diameter in millimetres, so the smaller sizes will have low numbers, such as 2.5mm, and the larger ones high numbers, such as 9mm (frequently used for the big, chunky blankets and throws popular in Sweden). But, if you are following an old pattern, you may find that needles are given a size based on a series of zeros ('0's, for example, 000). This was the old continental way of labelling needle sizes. The more '0's there are, the smaller the needle, until they reach size 2mm, which becomes size 1.

CASTING ON

Scandinavian knitting is often started with a decorative cast-on. This will not always curl up as would a cable or knitted cast-on, and many Scandinavian garments do not have a ribbed hem. The decorative cast-on can be worked with one or two colours. Make a slip knot with two ends of yarn; use one end from each ball, if using a contrast colour, or one long length about three times the length of yarn required for each stitch and one length coming from the ball, if using one colour only. Place the slip knot on the needle. Wrap the contrast-colour yarn or long length of yarn over the left thumb in a clockwise direction, as indicated. Insert the needle point in the manner indicated, under the loop on top of the thumb, and knit into the loop by using the other length of yarn. Pull slightly to tighten the resulting stitch on the needle. To cast on another stitch, again wrap the contrast-colour yarn or long length of yarn over the left thumb in a clockwise direction, and proceed as previously described. Continue as established until the appropriate number of stitches have been cast on with this long-tail, cast-on technique.

The slip knot that you made at the beginning of the cast-on is dropped from the needle at the end of the first row (or beginning of the first round) and doesn't count as a stitch. This method makes a flexible cast-on edge. For a sturdier and firmer edge, insert the needle under the lower strand of the loop on the thumb and bring it up in front of the upper strand before knitting it as described previously.

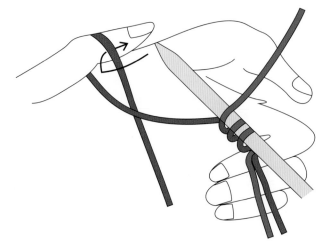

Working the long-tail cast-on.

Old Norwegian cast-on

This cast-on is similar to that produced by the method described above but makes a more stretchy and decorative edge.

Leaving a longer tail than you would expect (allowing for the yarn to wrap at least twice around the needle for each stitch of the cast-on), make a slip knot, and place it on the right-hand needle. In this case, it does count as the first stitch of the cast-on.

1. Place the thumb and index finger of your left hand between the yarn ends so that the strand connected to the ball is around your index finger and the tail end is around your thumb. Hold the rest of the yarn firmly in the palm of your left hand so that the yarn running from the thumb and from the index finger to the slip knot makes a 'V' shape.
2. Move the right-hand needle point from left to right under both strands of yarn around the thumb and then down from top to bottom into the centre of the thumb loop.
3. Move the right-hand needle forwards and upwards so that the yarn around the thumb is twisted.
4. Move the right-hand needle point from left to right to go over the closest part of the loop around the index finger and then under this part of the loop, to catch the yarn.
5. Bring the right-hand needle point back down through the bottom part of the thumb loop, below where the strands are crossed.
6. Drop the thumb loop off of your thumb, and tighten the resulting stitch on the right-hand needle.
7. Reposition the yarn around the thumb and index finger as described in step 1, and repeat steps 2–6 to cast on another stitch.
8. Repeat step 7 until the required number of stitches have been cast on.

Provisional cast-on

There may be times when you want what appears to be a seamless join between two pieces of knitting; for example, when joining two ends of a scarf so that they lie in the same direction and are mirror images of one another, requiring the scarf to be knitted in two directions, or when starting to work a saddle shoulder on a fisherman's sweater. The easiest method is to use a crochet hook to form and place the stitches on to the needle.

1. With waste yarn and using a crochet hook of the same size as the knitting needles that you will be using, make a slip knot, and place it on the hook.
2. Take one of your needles of the correct size, and hold it to the left of the crochet hook.
3. Take the yarn behind the needle, and reach for it with the crochet hook, by moving the hook over the top of the needle and to the left.
4. Pull the yarn through the loop on the crochet hook, making one stitch upon the needle.
5. Maintaining the positioning of the hook and needle (with the needle to the left of the hook), take the yarn behind the needle again, and repeat steps 3–4 until you have cast on as many stitches as you need.
6. Reach for the yarn with the crochet hook, pull the yarn all the way through the loop on the hook and leave a long yarn tail, to temporarily secure the yarn and be ready for you to undo the chain, to later gain access to live stitches.

With the yarn to be used for the pattern, work into the provisional-cast-on stitches on the needle. When the time comes to gain access to the stitches at the cast-on end of the knitted piece, first pull the long yarn tail back through the last loop of the provisional cast-on chain, then undo the cast-on chain one stitch or two stitches at a time from the tail end, and slip the live stitches on to your needle.

Alternatively, make a crochet chain with waste yarn, comprising at least as many chains as stitches required for the cast-on. Again, secure the end of the chain as described in step 6, leaving a long tail at the end of the chain. Pick up the 'bumps' at the back of the chain on to your needle, until you have the required number of cast-on stitches on the needle. Work into these bumps with the yarn to be used for the pattern, to form the first row (or round) of knitting. Undo the provisional cast-on and gain access to the live stitches as described previously, starting from the tail end of the cast-on chain.

Saddle shoulder
One use of a provisional cast-on is for the working of saddle shoulders for garments. This type of shoulder was frequently used for the simple shape of fishermen's sweaters, to add some extra room at the neck edge.

Leave the shoulder stitches of the back and front 'live'. Begin at the neck edge with a provisional cast-on, adding however many stitches you need for the width of the shoulder strap. As you knit the strap, work the last stitch together with one stitch from the adjacent shoulder. Once all of the shoulder stitches are used, continue knitting the sleeve. After the sleeve is finished, undo the stitches of the provisional cast on and slip them on to the needle for the knitting of the neckband.

CASTING OFF

A loose cast-off is often useful at the neck edge, especially in a basic tube-shaped garment with no neck shaping.

Stretchy cast-off

This method gives a more stretchy finish than the usual cast-off version of passing one stitch over the next one.

*Knit the first two stitches on the left-hand needle together, then slip the resulting stitch on the right-hand needle to the left-hand needle. Repeat from * to the end of the row (or round).

Alternatively, cast off each stitch with the usual cast-off method, working with a needle that is at least one size larger than the needles used to work the knitted fabric.

I-cord cast-off

At the end of working the piece, finish with the right side facing and keeping the yarn attached to the right-hand side of the fabric, then:

1. Cast on 3 stitches.
2. Knit the first 2 stitches on the left-hand needle, and then knit the third stitch on the left-hand needle together with the adjacent live stitch, closest to the point of the left-hand needle. (For the first round of the I-cord, first the second and third stitches that were cast on are knitted and then the first stitch that was cast on is knitted.)
3. Slip the 3 stitches on the right-hand needle on to the point of the left-hand needle, and repeat from step 2.

This makes a nice decorative edge at the neckline or at the cuff of a toe-up sock.

SOCKS AND STOCKINGS

A stretchy cast-on is best for socks worked from the cuff downwards. Use the long-tail option described previously, worked with a needle that is a size larger than that used for working the rest of the sock, and using either a single colour or, for a braid-like effect, two contrasting colours.

For a toe-up sock, either of the following two options can be used to start the toe.

Crochet start

1. Work 8 double-crochet stitches into a loop of yarn wound around the thumb (for example, by using the magic loop, or magic ring, technique). Join the stitches into a ring by slip stitching into the first stitch (this slip stitch does not count as a stitch).
2. Place the loop on the crochet hook on to a double-pointed needle; this loop counts as the first stitch. Continue by picking up 7 more stitches around the ring, starting with the second double-crochet stitch, by inserting the needle below the horizontal 'V' of each of the remaining crochet stitches in turn around the ring and drawing the yarn through, using two or three additional double-pointed needles as necessary to allow the stitches to remain in a circular arrangement. Pull on the tail end of the yarn to close this circle of stitches for the start of the toe.
3. Knit 1 round, then increase on alternate rounds in the usual way or as otherwise directed by the pattern until there are the required number of stitches for the foot.

When the sock is finished, firmly weave in the yarn end at the start of the toe so that the initial ring of crochet stitches stays closed.

Wrapped cast-on

1. Pull out a length of yarn and, using two needles held together in parallel, with one needle at the front and one at the back, first wrap the yarn tail around the needle held at the back, then wrap the yarn around the front needle, with the yarn following the course of a figure of eight.

2. Continue wrapping the yarn alternately around the back needle and then the front needle in this figure-of-eight course, until you have the required number of stitches present on the needles.

3. Turn the needles around so that the one that was at the back is now at the front, and, with the working end of the yarn, knit the stitches on the new front needle and then the stitches from the other needle, to form the first round of knitted stitches of the toe.

Heels

Scandinavian stockings were invariably worked from the cuff downwards and with a basic square heel and gusset.

1. Divide the live stitches so that one half the stitches are left for the instep and the other half are for making the heel flap. Note that only the heel-flap stitches will be worked in steps 2–3.

2. Knit the required number of rows over the heel-flap half of the stitches, based on the suggested proportions in the 'Example of working a stocking' information box in Chapter 3, slipping the first stitch of every row.

3. Next, turn the heel by working short rows. Knit across the row until about one third of the stitches on the needle are left unworked. Note the number of unworked stitches, then k2tog, k1 and turn. Turn, then purl across the row until the same number of unworked stitches are left at the end of this row, then p2tog, p1 and turn. Repeat by working across the central group of stitches in stocking stitch and then working the relevant k2tog, k1 and turn or p2tog, p1 and turn sequence, until all of the unworked stitches at the ends of the needle are used up.

4. Work around all of the stitches of the sock, including those left for the instep, by picking up each slipped stitch in turn along the sides of the heel flap when necessary (the stitches will be worked in the following order: stitches of one side of the heel flap, instep stitches, stitches of the other side of the heel flap and stitches of the heel flap). To get back to the original number of stitches, shape the gusset by working two stitches together at each side of the heel flap on alternate rows.

A useful way to work a heel that facilitates repair is to work an afterthought heel. This is worked in a similar manner to the thumb on a mitten. Work across the stitches for the instep, then knit the heel stitches with waste yarn. Place those stitches worked with waste yarn on to the left-hand needle, and work across them with the main yarn. Continue working until the sock is complete. Carefully remove the waste yarn, and pick up the live stitches that are exposed on to four double-pointed needles, then shape them as for a toe.

Toes

There are many different types of toe that are used for socks and stockings. Two of the most common types are described in the following sections.

Star toe

The star toe, also known as the beanie-shaped toe, is worked by decreasing evenly across the stitches of the round on every second or third round, with the last round being worked as k2tog to the end of the round. Leaving a short tail, cut the yarn, thread the yarn through the remaining stitches, draw up the yarn firmly, to gather the stitches together, and fasten off.

Wedge toe

With the stitches being divided equally over four double-pointed needles, a wedge toe is worked by decreasing at the end of the first needle, the beginning of the second, the end of the third and the beginning of the fourth on alternate rounds. When there are six stitches left on each needle, transfer the stitches so that there are twelve stitches on each of two needles, held in parallel, and either, with the right sides facing, cast off the first stitch on both needles together, then cast off the next pair of stitches on the front and back needles, and so on (a three-needle cast-off), or, with the wrong sides facing, graft the stitches on the front and back needles together with Kitchener stitch, to make a smooth seam.

A yoke of a Norwegian cardigan; photographed by Jon-Erik Faksvaag/Norsk Folkemuseum.

A Fair Isle hat with graduated colours.

FAIR ISLE OR SCANDINAVIAN?

The featured cardigan is an example of a Scandinavian design that sometimes incorporates three colours in a row for the large motifs, while the featured hat is an example of a Fair Isle design and shows how the colours are graduated throughout the pattern and two colours only are incorporated in any one row. While many of the shapes and motifs appear the same, there are some noticeable differences between the two techniques. Fair Isle knitting only ever includes two colours in a row but usually uses many colours, up to seven, within a single motif.

Fair Isle motifs were usually designed so that there would not be long strands of yarn (floats) between motifs; seven was frequently the maximum number of stitches permitted between the changes of colour. While the same approach could also be applied to many Scandinavian designs, long changes of colour can frequently be seen in several traditional patterns.

The Scandinavian knitters usually worked a motif in a single colour, often with bands of smaller motifs between them in a similar layout to that used by the Fair Isle knitters, who used their peerie (meaning 'small') patterns between motifs.

Many of these small patterns are the same across many knitting cultures, mainly because of the geometric nature of the stitches that naturally lends itself to the depiction of zigzags, small squares, crosses and diamonds. Note the row of hearts at the lower edge of the featured image, the same as those of the hearts border in the stitch dictionary in Chapter 6.

TWINED KNITTING

The technique of twined, or two-end, knitting (*tvåänds-stickning* or *twandstickning*) is very different to that of stranded colourwork, although again two strands of yarn are used at the same time. For this technique, the yarns are not carried across the back as floats that are caught in every few stitches but are twisted together after each stitch is worked, which forms a row of slanted stitches on the wrong side. The finished piece is thick, warm and fairly stiff. This technique can be worked with two colours but is more often seen with purled stitches on the right side that form geometric patterns.

As the strands of yarn are carried over each other in the same direction each time that the yarns are changed, they gradually become twisted together and eventually almost impossible to knit with. To remedy this, insert a

A single-colour, rounded-snowflake motif.

Fair Isle motifs, demonstrating their similarity to some Scandinavian designs.

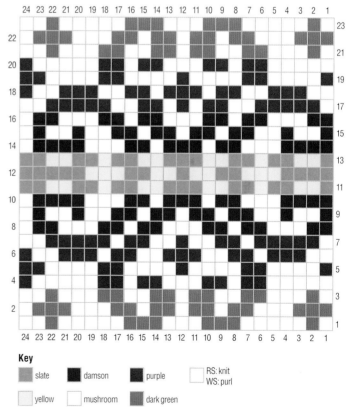

Key

▦ slate	■ damson
□ yellow	□ mushroom

■ purple	□ RS: knit / WS: purl
▦ dark green	

A chart for a snowflake motif to be worked with the Fair Isle technique.

A small sample of a diamond motif worked with the twined-knitting technique.

finger between the strands, nearest to the balls of yarn, so that they become more tightly entwined, then lift up the balls together, to allow the knitting to become suspended, and let the yarns slowly untwist themselves as the knitting rotates. Alternatively, let the yarns untwist at the ball end by inserting a stick or pencil through the balls so that they don't unwind, and then lift up the knitting, to allow the balls to become suspended, and let the yarns slowly untwist themselves as the balls rotate. Because of the necessity to regularly untwist the yarns, it is easy to see why this technique was usually used for small items such as mittens, socks and hats and why I have used it for a pair of wristlets featured in Chapter 4.

THRUMS

One other method of making a warm fabric is to layer wool on the inside of the garment by catching in short strands of roving, or unspun wool, that are usually a little thicker than the working yarn, on the wrong side of the fabric. Pull out a few lengths of the unspun wool measuring about 8–10cm (3–4in), then shape each length into a ring by overlapping the ends a little. Twist the centre of each ring so that it is of about the same

thickness as of the knitting yarn: this twisted ring of unspun wool is called a 'thrum'. Work one or two stitches of the fabric with the main yarn, insert the right-hand needle into the next stitch on the left-hand needle, then, instead of wrapping the working yarn around the right-hand needle to knit the next stitch, place one of your thrums on to the right-hand needle so that both ends of the thrum are at the back of the work and the centre is sitting on the needle point, creating a loop that is formed by the thrum wrapping around the needle. Knit the stitch into which the right-hand needle is inserted by now wrapping the yarn around the tip of the needle and around the thrum loop and then pulling both the thrum loop and the wrapped yarn through the stitch on the left-hand needle. Continue working in pattern until you reach the next stitch where a thrum is to be placed, and again position the thrum and work the stitch to receive the thrum as described.

On the next row, knit the thrum and the main yarn of the thrummed stitch together. On the right side of your work, you will have a thicker, larger stitch; often, the unspun yarn used for the thrums is of a contrast colour, resulting in a contrast-colour stitch on the right side of the knitting. On the wrong side of the knitting will be the ends of your soft thrum. These thrum ends will gradually felt together as the accessory or garment is worn and washed, making a nice thick lining for, for example, some very cosy mittens.

FINISHING

When all of the knitting is done, the knitted fabric will look even better if it is blocked. If your garment has been made in pieces, not in the round, the sewing up will be easier if the pieces are blocked first. There are two main methods: wet blocking and steam blocking.

Wet blocking

Dampen each piece with lukewarm water, but not so that they are dripping wet, and spread them out on a towel or blocking board. You need to be able to leave them in place, undisturbed, until they are dry, which can sometimes take twenty-four hours! While the pieces are in place, gently pull each piece into the shape and the measurements required for that piece and pin it (with rustproof pins) at the edges.

The wrong side of a piece of thrummed knitting.

The thrums as they look on the outside, or right side, of a piece of thrummed knitting.

Steam blocking

The pieces are not wet first but are pinned out to the required shape and measurements on top of a towel or on an ironing board. Either use a steam iron by hovering it over the pieces so that the steam is forced through them or lay a dampened, clean cloth over the pieces and lightly press them with an iron. Do check the ball band of the yarn used to knit the pieces for the appropriate temperature setting to use.

Sewing up

If you have worked the garment in pieces and need to join them together, the tidiest way to form the seams is by using mattress stitch.

Join in yarn matching the colour and thickness of the project yarn (preferably some of the yarn used to knit the project pieces) to the bottom edge of the pieces to be joined and, with right sides uppermost and lying side by side, take a needle threaded with this yarn under the first two horizontal strands running between the first and second stitches in from the edge of the right-hand piece, across to the left-hand piece and then under the first two horizontal strands running between the first and second stitches in from the edge of the left-hand piece. Continue working from side to side, periodically pulling the edges of the pieces together by pulling on both the yarn end at the start of the seam and the yarn threaded into the needle, to form a closed, tight seam, as you work along the seam.

If you have knitted your garment in the round then all you need to do is join the shoulders with a three-needle cast-off, or graft them together, darn in any loose yarn ends and pull the garment on to wear it!

Sewing up ribbing

The neatest edge is formed when a k1 p1 rib is started with two knit stitches. Use mattress stitch, but take the needle under the centre of the second knit stitch each time. This will give an edge that looks like one knit stitch.

Mattress stitch.

CHAPTER 3

NORWAY

You would think, given its geographical location, that Norwegians had been knitting themselves warm, woollen clothing for thousands of years, but this is not the case; it is a relatively new craft there and was not widely practised until the mid-nineteenth century. It is claimed by the Norsk Folkemuseum that the first knitted clothing in Norway was that of the night-shirt or *nattroje* that was also widely used in Denmark. This type of garment was worn as underwear as well as for when in bed, and it was usually made of silk, in a single colour, covered in a brocade or damask pattern of knit and purl stitches. This pattern was most often of small stars arranged over the fabric, such as the one featured here.

These silk garments were most probably imported as finished items from Italy in the seventeenth century, probably being worn only by royalty. Later, as the design became adopted more generally, they were knitted locally for outdoor wear and were made from wool. Women would make them for their own families but also to sell, in order to add to the family income. They were of a very basic shape similar to that of a fisherman's gansey, knitted in the round as a tube for the body with openings being cut out for the sleeves. The sleeves would be knit from the cuff upwards, also in the round, and then sewn into place at the armholes. Unlike the typical fisherman's gansey worn around the coasts of the British Isles, there were no underarm gussets in these Scandinavian garments.

A Norwegian fjord.

The early versions of these Norwegian sweaters were usually patterned only on the upper part of the body, as they were worn under the dungarees-type outfit that the men wore for working. If they had any colourwork sections, it would be on the yoke only; the rest of the garment was plain white. Patterning on the upper body is frequently seen in garments intended as workwear, as it is easier to repair such garments as they become worn if they are plainly knitted.

A set of stars, typically used on Danish nightshirts or nattrojer.

A typical fishermen's gansey, showing the underarm gussets and tube-like construction.

A jacket, possibly from the Fana region of Norway, where this pattern of dotted stripes was used extensively on many styles of garment. Knitting and Crochet Guild.

With its long stretch of coast, there were naturally many fishing ports, and wherever there are fishermen there appears to be the ubiquitous fisherman's gansey. Norwegian fishermen were no exception, although their version differed slightly in that it often had bands of white stars or snowflakes along the shoulder edges. The rest of the garment would be made as a tube of either plain knitting or a small, all-over, geometric pattern.

As elsewhere, these garments were knitted in the round. In some cases, there was a half gusset at each underarm that was not decreased down into the sleeves as on a gansey but was used in place of the more familiar cast-off section of stitches.

Similarly shaped garments to these also were worn by farmworkers and men working on the land in the forests. The inclusion of different stitches can actually change the properties of a knitted fabric, and including purl stitches on a plain background makes for a slightly thicker, and therefore warmer, piece of fabric, which is very desirable in these chilly northern areas. The yarn forming the purl stitches travels a greater distance around the needle than does the yarn forming the knit stitches, resulting in little pockets that trap air. While the garment would traditionally be made as a tube, as explained above, I have designed this one in a more modern shape, working the back and the front separately, with set-in sleeves and a crew neckline.

FOREST SWEATER

Swedish pines.

Size

To fit a chest circumference of 36 (40, 44, 48)in
Actual measurements: chest circumference 38 (42, 47, 51)in; back length 24 (25, 25, 26)in; sleeve-seam length 18 (19, 19½, 20)in

Materials

500 (600, 650, 700)g of light aran-weight yarn

Needles

1 pair 4.5mm needles
1 pair 3.5mm needles
Circular 3.5mm needle

Tension

20sts and 24 rows to 10cm/4in using 4.5mm needles over st. st

The forest sweater – is a chunky, thick sweater suitable for country walks.

Back

Using 3.5mm needles, cast on 96 (104, 112, 120)sts, and work 2½in of k2, p2 rib.
Inc to 97 (105, 113, 121)sts on last row.

Change to 4.5mm needles, and cont in st. st until work measures 14 (15, 16, 17)in from cast-on edge, ending with RS facing, having completed a WS row.

Armhole shaping and yoke patterning
Cast off 5 (5, 6, 6)sts at beg of next 2 rows.
Dec by 1 stitch at each end of every alt row until 81 (89, 89, 97)sts rem, working in patt as follows:
Next row (RS): Purl.
Next row (WS): Purl.
Next row: Knit.
Next row: Knit.
Next row: Knit.
Next row: Purl.
Next row: Purl.
Next row: Purl.
Work from brocade chart until armholes measure 8½ (9, 9½, 9¾)in, ending with RS facing, having completed a WS row.

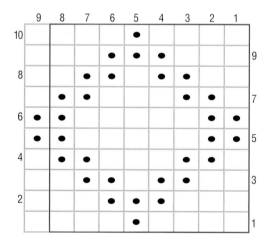

The brocade chart for the forest sweater.

Shoulder shaping

Cast off 8 (9, 9, 9)sts at beg of next 4 rows and 9 (9, 9, 10) sts at beg of next 2 rows.
Slip 31 (35, 37, 41)sts on to a holder for back neck.

Front

Work as for back until armholes measure 6 (6¼, 6½, 6¾)in.

Neck shaping

Patt 33 (36, 35, 38)sts, slip 15 (17, 19, 21)sts on to a holder for front neck, patt to end.
Dec by 1 stitch at neck edge of every row until 25 (27, 27, 28)sts rem.
When armhole measures the same length as for that of the back, shape shoulder as for back.
Return to rem 33 (36, 35, 38)sts, for left front, and work these sts as for right front.

Sleeves

Using 3.5mm needles, cast on 46 (46, 52, 56)sts, and work 3in of k2, p2 rib.
Change to 4.5mm needles, and cont in st. st, increasing at each end of every 8th row until there are 66 (72, 78, 84)sts.
Work even in st. st until piece measures 18 (19, 19½, 20)in from cast-on edge, ending with RS facing, having completed a WS row.

Sleeve-cap shaping

Cast off 5 (5, 6, 7)sts at beg of next 2 rows until 56 (62, 66, 70)sts rem.
Dec by 1 stitch at each end of next 2 (4, 5, 5) rows until 52 (54, 58, 60)sts rem and then every alt row until 24 (24, 30, 32)sts rem.
Dec by 1 stitch at each end of next 2 (4, 4, 5) rows.
Cast off loosely.

Work second sleeve as for first sleeve.

Join shoulders with Kitchener stitch or three-needle cast-offs.

A sunny but chilly day, ideal for the wearing of the forest sweater.

Neckband

Using a 3.5mm circular needle, knit across 31 (35, 37, 41)sts from back-neck holder, pick up and knit 22 (23, 23, 25)sts along left-front neck edge, knit 15 (17, 19, 21)sts from front-neck holder and pick up and knit 22 (23, 23, 25)sts along right-front neck edge. [90 (98, 102, 112)sts]
Work 8 rows of k2, p2 rib.
Cast off loosely in patt.

Finishing

Set in sleeves to separate armholes. Sew both side seams and sleeve seams, and weave in all yarn ends.

ANNEMOR SUNDBØ

In 1983, Annemor Sundbø, a textile designer and weaver, wanted to learn more about the techniques of weaving pieces in a small mill. She approached the owner of the Torridal Tweed mill near Kristiansand and asked him to teach her about small-scale mill weaving. He agreed that he would, on condition that she bought the mill! Annemor thought that this would be an opportunity not to be missed, and so she agreed to purchase the mill and everything in it. Upon going through the various rooms, she discovered a pile of items waiting to be turned into shoddy, the specialty of the mill. 'Shoddy' is a term that we associate now with poorly made, inferior products, but the term originally actually referred to a product made from recycled fibres. The garments were shredded and mixed with small amounts of new wool and then woven into a cheap cloth that could be used for making military uniforms and work clothes. It was also known as rag wool

and was a cheap yarn for making everyday stockings and the like. When Annemor found this pile of rags, she realized that they represented a history of traditional Norwegian knitting. This discovery encouraged her to investigate further, and she travelled around the area, collecting stories, photographs and newspaper articles. The descriptions from the local knitters were full of tales of the symbolism of the knitting motifs and the folk tales surrounding them. She felt that these were too important to Norway to be lost and, in 2001, published the book *Everyday Knitting*, containing ideas and inspiration alongside several patterns representing Norway's cultural history. She went on to produce other books on Norwegian knitting, including one about the pictorial representation of knitting in art, more about which is covered in Chapter 5, and another on the history of sweaters from Setesdal, including the famous *Lusekofte* (lice jacket).

Another item from the Knitting and Crochet Guild's Collection. It is possibly machine knitted and is trimmed with embroidery. It is very like the Marius design (Mariusgenser) from Dale of Norway.

LUSEKOFTE SWEATERS

Adding another layer of yarn to a sweater would provide even more warmth to the wearer than would a single-layer sweater, and the thicker layer of fabric would provide some wind resistance. *Lusekofte* incorporate such a double layer of yarn. Many garments would be knitted with two colours of yarn, with the body having a pattern of small spots and the yoke a more elaborate set of motifs, as in the pattern featured here, inspired by the *Lusekofte* of the Setesdal region of southern Norway. It is said to be the pattern that is most knitted throughout the world. It was probably first made in the early part of the twentieth century, and this uniquely patterned sweater was 'discovered' by tourists, just as the sweaters of the Aran Islands were so 'discovered'. The little lice pattern was used to add an extra layer of yarn to the sweater without too much complication. It could easily be worked by any half-competent knitter and parts of a garment to include this pattern were often given to the children to work, while the adults completed the more complex parts of the design.

The most familiar design would have the lower half worked in these spots of contrast colour (usually white on black), familiarly known as 'lice', then bands of small motifs such as upside-down triangles followed by a divider of alternate stripes, then a medium-sized pattern, perhaps small

An example of the embroidered bands frequently used to trim the neck and sometimes the cuffs of many Norwegian sweaters.

Norwegian clasps, used to fasten the neckline of the sweater, in place of buttons and buttonholes.

diamonds and/or crosses, then another set of dividing stripes, then a large motif of diamonds and crosses and often some chevrons at the shoulder edges to finish.

Many of these traditional garments would have their neck edges and the cuffs decorated with fabric bands of bright embroidery and the openings finished with silver clasps rather than buttons, which is a handy way of avoiding the making of buttonholes.

The garments often incorporated red bands or facings. When Norway was occupied by Germany in 1940, many Norwegians showed their solidarity and resistance to this occupation by wearing red caps, a popular item of headgear throughout Scandinavia. These caps were banned by the Germans in 1942, and so many knitters introduced sections of red into their knitwear instead.

The featured pattern that I have designed is based on a traditional *Lusekofte* of black and white with bands of red. This modern version is worked with a main yarn that has a gradual colour change rather than with spots being worked on the lower body. However, there is no reason why you could not convert it into a more traditional-looking *Lusekofte* by adding your own 'lice'.

RIGHT: *This sweater design was inspired by the well-known* Lusekofte *of Norway.*

LUSEKOFTE-INSPIRED SWEATER

With its clasps rather than buttons, this is a unisex garment, as you can see from the featured photographs, but if you want to add buttons then, traditionally, they should be made of pewter.

Size

To fit a chest circumference of 36 (42)in
Actual measurements: chest circumference 38½ (44½)in; back length 24 (25)in; sleeve length 17½ (19½)in

Materials

4 (5) × 100g balls of James C Brett Landscape DK yarn; 20-per-cent wool, 80-per-cent acrylic (260m[284yd]/100g) in Charcoal (MC)
1 (1) × 100g ball of James C Brett Landscape DK yarn; 20-per-cent wool, 80-per-cent acrylic (260m[284yd]/100g) in White (CC1)
0.5 (0.5) × 100g ball of James C Brett Landscape DK yarn; 20-per-cent wool, 80-per-cent acrylic (260m[284yd]/100g) in Red (CC2)

Needles

Circular 3.25mm needle
Circular 4mm needle
1 pair 4mm needles
3 Norwegian clasps

Tension

22sts and 28 rows to 10cm/4in using 4mm needles over st. st

Body

Worked in the round as one piece as far as split for armholes.
Using a circular 3.25mm needle and MC, cast on 212 (240)sts. Join to work in the round, taking care not to twist the stitches. Work k1, p1 rib for 2½in.
Mark the position of the side 'seams', at beg of round and at halfway point of round, after the 106th (120th) stitch. Change to a circular 4mm needle, and work Chart A. When Chart A is completed, cont in st. st with MC until work measures 8 (9)in from cast-on edge. Work Chart B, and, at the same time, when piece measures 14 (15) in from cast-on edge, divide for the armholes: transfer the just-completed 106 (120)sts at beg of round to a holder for front.

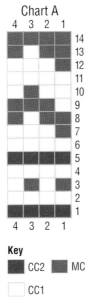

Chart A

Key

CC2   MC

CC1

RIGHT: *The chart for the Lusekofte-inspired sweater.*

Chart B

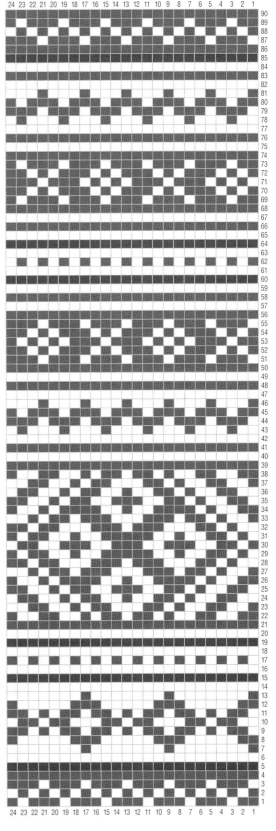

A close-up of the yoke and sleeve patterns of the Lusekofte-*inspired sweater.*

The back of the Lusekofte-*inspired sweater.*

Back

Using a pair of 4mm needles, work back and forth on back section only, starting with RS facing and resuming working from Chart B at relevant row to cont in patt.

Work Chart B to end or, if necessary, rep Chart B rows until piece reaches length required.

Shoulder shaping

Cast off 32 (37)sts at beg of next 2 rows, or leave these sts on a holder for later working of a three-needle cast-off.

Place rem 42 (46)sts (for back neck) on to a holder.

Front

Divide for front opening.

Return to working 106 (120)sts on front holder, and resume working from Chart B at relevant row to cont in patt; with RS facing, patt across 46 (53)sts from front holder (for left front), cast off 14 (16)sts, patt to end (for right front).

Cont working from Chart B on set of sts for right front until armhole measures 5½in.

Neck shaping

Cast off 8sts at neck edge of next row.

Dec by 1 stitch at neck edge of next 5 rows and then following 3 alt rows. [30 (37)sts]

Cont working from Chart B until armhole measures same as for back.

Cast off 30 (37)sts for shoulder, or cast them off together with those of the back (with a three-needle cast-off).

Work left front as for right front.

Join shoulders with Kitchener stitch, if not already joined by three-needle cast-offs.

Sleeves

Worked in the round.

With RS facing and using a circular 4mm needle, pick up and knit 98 (106)sts around one armhole edge, beginning from the underarm (where the back and front divide).

Work Chart C, ensuing that full pattern repeats will be positioned as mirror images on left and right sleeves, and, at

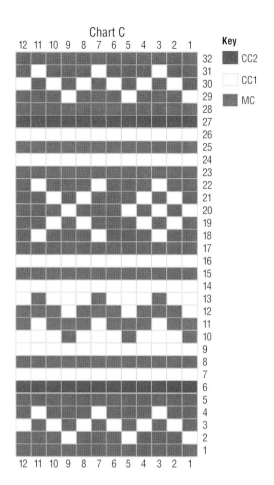

Chart C

12 11 10 9 8 7 6 5 4 3 2 1

Key
- CC2
- CC1
- MC

The chart for the sleeve of Lusekofte-*inspired sweater.*

The yoke of the Lusekofte-*inspired sweater.*

The Lusekofte-*inspired sweater, with its red neckband lining.*

the same time, dec at each end of every 4th round.

Change to MC, cont in st. st and dec at each end of every 4th round until 42 (50)sts rem.

Work even in st. st until piece measures 15 (17)in from armhole edge.

Change to a circular 3.25mm needle, and work k1, p1 rib for 2½in, then cast off loosely in patt.

Work second sleeve as for first sleeve.

Neckband

Using a circular 3.25mm needle and MC, with RS facing, pick up and knit 8sts from right-front neck-edge cast-off, pick up and knit 14 (16)sts along right-front neck edge, knit 42 (46)sts from back-neck holder, pick up and knit 14 (16) sts along left-front neck edge and pick up and knit 8sts from left-front neck-edge cast-off. [86 (94)sts]

With WS facing, knit across row.

Work rows 58–66 of Chart B.

With MC, with WS facing, knit across row, to form neckband fold line.

The finished Lusekofte-inspired sweater.

Happy to be wearing such an attractive sweater!

Work 11 rows of st. st with CC2. Cast off loosely.

Front bands

For right-front band, using a circular 3.25mm needle and MC, with RS facing, pick up and knit 40sts along vertical right-front edge, until reaching fold line of neckband. Work as for neckband. Cast off loosely.

For left-front band, using a circular 3.25mm needle and MC, with RS facing, pick up and knit 40sts along vertical left-front edge, starting from fold line of neckband. Work as for neckband. Cast off loosely.

Fold neckband and each front band in half along its fold line, and hem each band in place on WS of fabric.

Finishing

Sew on Norwegian clasps to left- and right-front bands. Weave in all yarn ends.

EVOLUTION OF NORWEGIAN KNITWEAR

The spotted jerseys are the items that most people think of as being typically Norwegian and are often described as ski jumpers. However, they are actually fairly modern, probably first made in the twentieth century.

Another style that has been around since the nineteenth century but has become more popular today is that of the sweaters from the Fana region on the west coast of Norway. They also incorporate 'lice' but this time between bands of blue or black, alternated with bands of lice on a white background. They often have a chequerboard pattern in the same colours at the hem and a band of stars or roses at the shoulders and cuffs. When such a garment was made as a cardigan, which it frequently was for women, the front edges were often trimmed with embroidered braid.

The majority of knitted pieces held by the Norsk Folkemuseum are not outer garments but underwear, stockings and mittens.

The featured mittens were donated to the Alta Museum by Liv Brygfjeld (1901–1987), maiden name Kummeneje. Her father was Johannes H. Kummeneje, a local sheriff and member of parliament. Liv received the mittens from a family named Hofseth from Leirbotn, about a forty-minute drive from Alta. The Hofseths were related to Liv's husband, Ragnar Christensen Brygfjeld. According to the information provided by Liv, the mittens were made around 1879.

Bergen, on the west coast of Norway, was, and still is, an important centre for trade. Fish and furs were exported, and grain and clothing were imported, from as early as the eleventh century. This import of clothing may have been one of the ways in which knitted garments were seen and copied by the women of Norway. They would also be seen on the backs of the seamen, and there are similarities between the Breton striped shirts, the fishermen's ganseys, the Fair Isle-patterned jumpers of Britain and the yoked sweaters of Iceland.

The first printed knitting patterns in Norway were produced in the late nineteenth century. What were known as 'household' books, for example, *The Household Book for Town and Country*, included short sections on knitting, with a few patterns, especially for stockings, hats and underwear. There were also books of sampler patterns for girls to sew at school that were often used as a source of knitting motifs.

A pair of mittens held in the World Heritage Rock Art Centre – Alta Museum, photographed by Anne Klippenvåg Pettersen.

A hand-knitted cardigan, made in Scandinavia but held in the collection of the Knitting and Crochet Guild in the UK.

This jumper was knitted in Norway but commissioned by Tulloch of Shetland.

Craftspeople of all kinds are adept at visualizing patterns in different formats and will happily take elements of one craft to use in another. It is easy to see the influence of Fair Isle in the featured cardigan, knitted in Norway and donated to the Knitting and Crochet Guild.

NATIONAL IDENTITY

After 1905, when Norway became separate from Sweden, there was a distinct feeling that Norway should establish its own national identity.

Annichen Sibbern Bohn (1905–1978) was a collector of traditional patterns and, in 1927, toured Norway on behalf of the Norwegian Home Arts and Crafts organization (Husflid), collecting designs and making charts and patterns for her book *Norske Strikkemønstre*, or *Norwegian Knitting Designs*.

This atmosphere inspired women to feel national pride and to imbue their knitting with a sense of national identity. Folk costumes from various regions were examined, and colours and motifs that seemed to reflect the country were used more widely in knitwear.

Aagot Noss (1924–2015), curator at the Norsk Folkemuseum, was very interested in traditional folk costumes, and, during the 1950s, she travelled around Norway, documenting the traditional dress of the various regions. She wrote several books describing the different styles of dress and included pictures and drawings of the motifs found on them. These books were all sold in numerous copies, suggesting that they were used by knitters to create their own designs.

Red, white and blue – the colours of the Norwegian flag – were often employed in folk costumes, and knitted items were no exception. Three-year-old Prince Harald was shown to be wearing a set composed of a red-and-white knitted sweater, hat and mittens in a photograph taken before the family went into exile in the USA in 1940. This set is still in the possession of the royal family, and members of one of Norway's craft organizations recreated an adult version for Harald upon his accession to the throne in 1991.

MITTENS

In a country where large parts of it have cold, wet weather for most of the year, mittens are definitely a necessity. Early pairs were made from leather or from yarn worked with the technique of naalbinding. A pair dating from 1772 (with the date embroidered on the mitten) has been found and is preserved in the Røros Museum. The mittens are plain blue, knitted in stocking stitch and then embroidered later on with red and cream, to be given as a wedding gift. Many pairs of mittens have dates knitted into them, which suggests that they were intended as mementoes of various occasions. Until after the Second World War, it was the custom that every bride had to give a pair of mittens to all of the men attending the wedding as well as to give a pair of socks to the bridegroom and all of the members of his family!

An example of a cropped sweater with bands of diamonds worked in purl stitch on a plain background.
Item NF 1988-0070, photo: Haakon Harriss/Norsk Folkemuseum.

In 1901, Caroline Halvorsen published a book called *A Knitting Book for Schools and Home*; it covered the basic techniques of knitting and was used in schools in Norway until the 1960s. It didn't contain complete patterns but explained how to incorporate the various cables, motifs, palms and thumbs into a basic mitten pattern. It is not surprising that several museums in Norway each have in their collections pairs of mittens made from the same patterns. One of the designs has a band of Old Shale patterns down the back of the hand, flanked by small cables; this is a design that we would normally associate with the Shetland Islands, but it is not inconceivable that such designs were copied from earlier published books and leaflets.

Selbu mittens (*Selbuvotter*)

The Selburose is the motif that is internationally recognized as originating in Norway; however, it is actually a widespread and long-standing design used in many countries and cultures and was frequently used as a textured pattern for the Danish *nattrojer*. It actually resembles a star rather than a rose and is sometimes referred to as the Norwegian star. The rose or star motif appears on the earliest silk knitted garments to be found in Europe and on cushions found in a fourteenth-century grave in Spain; counted-thread embroidery worked on woven- or mesh-type fabrics lends itself to the presentation of geometric designs such as this, and patterns to be worked on knitted fabrics, which are also based on rectangles, can easily be interpreted from embroidery designs.

Most of the designs that we now identify with Norway, those of stars, snowflakes, fir trees and reindeer, originated in the small northern district of Selbu. These patterns are said to have been created there by a young girl called Marit Emstad (1841–1929) who worked on a local farm. One day, the farmer, Jo Kjosnes, saw one of the other milkmaids, Marit Guldseth, knitting a pair of stockings for her husband. These stockings had a pattern of black on white resembling a snake curling along the back of the leg. Jo asked Marit Emstad whether she could knit patterns like that too, and she said that she could. When she got home, she worked on a pair of mittens with an eight-pointed star on the back, possibly copied from a cross-stitch embroidery motif from one of the printed stitch-pattern books.

Marit and her sister wore their mittens to church, and, as any knitter would upon seeing an item or pattern that they liked, individuals present in the congregation decided to create their own similarly patterned mittens instead of the plain-white *naalbinding* ones that they usually wore. The knitters became more and more ambitious with their designs and often gave them names after the farms on which they lived or after members of their family. Some knitters even knitted motifs of reindeer or dogs into their mittens rather than the variations of the Selbu rose. They would work the upper hand and palms of the mittens with different patterns and were often very adventurous with the use of smaller patterns on the thumbs that, again, had a different pattern on the back. The patterns of the cuffs were usually different to those of the hand too, sometimes with leaves, flowers or little people, although the men's versions were usually less elaborate, with

Key
- ☐ MC
- ☐ RS: knit
  WS: purl
- ■ Petrol
- ▨ Sage

A Norwegian star, with border patterns above and below it, depicted on a chart.

small stars or stripes. Selbu mittens were often given as gifts to the bride and groom on their wedding day, and these mittens would often have inscriptions, such as 'congratulations' or the initials of the couple, knitted into them. But the mittens were also knitted for sale, and, gradually, the designs and patterns were written down and published, and there are now more than 500 different patterns registered as being for Selbuvotter.

In 2013, Anne Bårdsgård began collecting patterns from Selbu and organizing groups of knitters to make them, in readiness for the development and publication of her book, *Selbuvotter*. The mittens have also been displayed at travelling exhibitions around Norway, where they are set up on walls in the manner of an art exhibition. When their travels are complete, they will be kept in the Selbu Village Museum. All of Anne's mittens were knitted with black and white yarns, just like the first ones knitted by Marit Emstad, and followed the tradition of having lace or long (about four-inch) rib cuffs for the women's mittens and short rib or garter-stitch cuffs for the men's. The cuffs would often be striped, and this would form a chevron pattern on the lace ones. Like the patterns on the

upper hand and on the palm, there are hundreds of variations of the arrangement of the stripes. As an example, one pair of ladies' mittens begins with a version of the Razor Shell pattern:

Row 1: K1, *yo, k1, ssk, k1, yo, k1; rep from * to the end of the row.
Row 2: Knit.
A total of 12 rows are worked in white, then one row in black, one in white, two in black, one in white and one in black.

This sequence is repeated once, then there are two more rows of white before a pattern of little people holding hands is worked upside down, followed by a pattern of some small dogs in a row. Next comes a small geometric divider pattern, followed by the expected column of Selburose motifs, flanked by the flower-border motif of the mittens and headband patterns featured here. The thumb has a lovely little geometric design, reminiscent of wrought-iron work, topped by a pattern of a little girl. The palm is covered in a trellis pattern. The men's mittens also feature stars, flowers and little people, and all are beautifully knitted in wool from the Hillesvåg Ullvarefabrikk, a nineteenth-century mill near Bergen, or the local Selbu Spinneri, a small mill started in 2011. Both of these mills use wool from local sheep, but the Selbu mill aims to use that from rarer breeds.

In 1936, the American magazine *Ski Illustrated* published articles and illustrations of skiers wearing these mittens with the eight-pointed star design. Norway had exported thousands of these mittens from Selbu during the 1930s. They were referred to as sport mittens, and later editions of the magazine had an illustration of Sonja Henie (a Norwegian Olympic ice skater) wearing a pair. They gradually became known worldwide, and patterns, initially aimed at the winter-sports aficionado, were published in magazines such as *Needlecraft* and *Weldon's Practical Knitter*. As demand increased, the quality of the mittens gradually deteriorated. It was obviously quicker to produce them on larger needles and with thicker yarn and with less elaborate patterns. In 1934, the Selbu Handicrafts Council issued charts and instructions in an attempt to try to recover and maintain the quality that the early mittens had exhibited. The quality improved again, and, for the Olympic Games in 1960, the Norwegian athletes were each given a pair of Selbu mittens.

The pattern featured here is for a rose motif but, by using the blank chart provided in Chapter 7 as a design template and filling it in with your preferred motif, you can make a version of your own.

MITTENS AND MATCHING HEADBAND

Size

Mittens actual measurements: length (cuff to tip) 9½in; circumference 7in (to fit women's-size-small hands)

Headband actual measurements: depth 3in; circumference 17in

Materials

1 × 100g skein of Rowan Moordale yarn; 70-per-cent wool, 30-per-cent alpaca (230m[252yd]/100g) in MC

1 × 100g skein of Rowan Moordale yarn; 70-per-cent wool, 30-per-cent alpaca (230m[252yd]/100g) in contrast colour (CC)

Needles

Circular 3mm needle
Circular 4mm needle
4–5 double-pointed 4mm needles

Tension

26sts and 26 rows to 10cm/4in using 4mm needles over colourwork patt

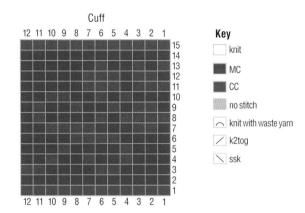

Cuff

| | | | | | | | | | | | | |
|12|11|10|9|8|7|6|5|4|3|2|1|

Key
- knit
- MC
- CC
- no stitch
- knit with waste yarn
- k2tog
- ssk

Rows: 15 14 13 12 11 10 9 8 7 6 5 4 3 2 1

ABOVE AND RIGHT: *The charts for the mittens and headband.*

Left mitten

Using a circular 3mm needle and holding both working yarns together (that is, with one length each of MC and CC), cast on 48sts.

Work 4 rounds of g. st with CC.

Change to a circular 4mm needle, and work cuff chart (15 rounds).

Work 4 rounds of g. st with CC.

Work 19 rounds by following mitten-upper-hand chart over first half of each round (24sts) and then mitten-palm chart over second half of each round (24sts).

Thumb placement

Next round: Work round 20 of mitten-upper-hand chart, work first 14sts of round 20 of mitten-palm chart and then knit 9sts with a length of waste yarn. Slip the 9 just-knitted stitches purlwise to left-hand needle, and knit them with MC. Knit to end of round as specified by mitten-palm chart. Cont following mitten-upper-hand and mitten-palm charts, shaping the top of the mitten as indicated, until 10sts rem.

Right mitten

Work as for left mitten until second section of g. st has been completed.

Work 19 rounds by following mitten-palm chart over first half of each round (24sts) and then mitten upper-hand chart over second half of each round (24sts).

Cosy to wear!

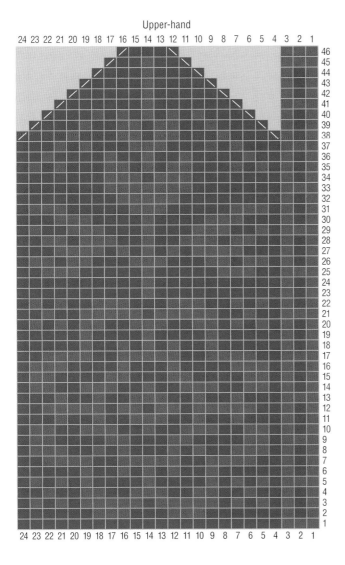

Upper-hand

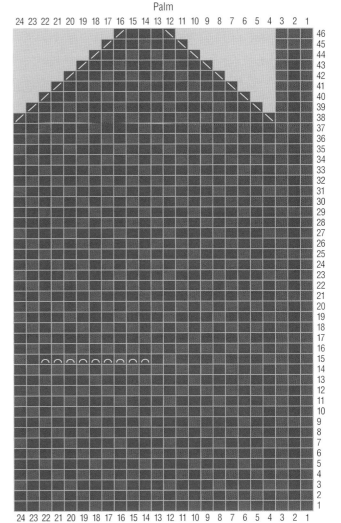

Palm

Thumb placement

Next round: Work first 4sts of round 20 of mitten-palm chart and then knit 9sts with a length of waste yarn. Slip the 9 just-knitted stitches purlwise to left-hand needle, and knit them with MC. Work next 11sts of round 20 of mitten-palm chart and then work round 20 of upper-hand chart. Cont following mitten-palm and mitten-upper-hand charts, shaping top of mitten as indicated, until 10sts rem.

Thumbs

Remove waste yarn carefully from first mitten, and slip the 9 live stitches from lower edge and upper edge of the resulting opening on to 3 or 4 double-pointed 4mm needles. With MC, beginning at stitch closest to centre of palm, knit 1 round, and, at the same time, pick up and knit 1 stitch from

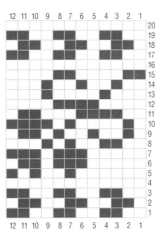

The flower-border chart could be used as an alternative to the mitten-cuff chart or you could design your own cuff pattern, if desired.interesting shapes and motifs.

A view showing the palm and thumb of the mittens, as well as the upper-hand pattern.

each end of the lower and upper edges (that is, between the two sets of 9 live stitches). (20sts)

Pm after 10th stitch of round, to designate upper and lower sides of thumb (10sts each).

Work 1 round of k1 MC, k1 CC, then work 1 round of k1 CC, k1 MC. Next, work only stitches 10–19 of rounds 37–46 of the mitten upper-hand chart over the stitches of each side of the thumb (that is, on each round, the indicated stitches will be worked once before and once after the marker).

After thumb measures 2in, with MC only, k2tog around for 2 rounds.

Leaving a tail, cut the yarn, thread the yarn through the rem sts, draw up sts, to close the hole at the top of the thumb, and fasten off.

Weave in all yarn ends.

Headband

Using a circular 3mm needle and holding both working yarns together (that is, with one length each of MC and CC), cast on 96sts.

A view of the headband, with its pattern echoing that on the cuff of the mittens.

The headband keeping ears cosy.

Work 4 rounds of g. st with CC.
Change to a circular 4mm needle, and work mitten-cuff chart (15 rounds).
Work 4 rounds of g. st with CC.
Cast off with MC.

Weave in all yarn ends.

SELBU STAR

The Selbu star, or Selburose, in its various adaptations, is now seen as the typical Norwegian motif and appears on everything from hats to stockings, sweaters and even statues, as well as, most numerously, the famous mittens. Once the sport of skiing came into fashion in the Nordic countries and in central Europe, the Selbu mittens very soon became an important export product. The mittens were sold all over Europe and

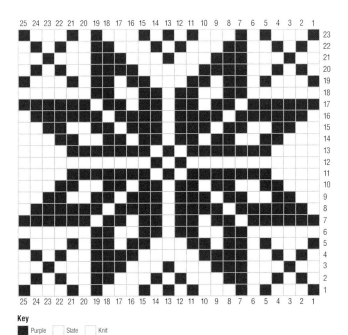

Key

■ Purple ☐ Slate ☐ Knit

A chart for the Norwegian star or Selburose pattern.

Did you know?

In 2008, knitters in Selbu knitted a huge pair of mittens that appeared in the *Guinness Book of Records* in 2014 as the biggest pair of Selbu mittens in the world.

the USA. The Norwegian Olympic teams were equipped with them in 1960, as were the members of the Belgian expeditions to the South Pole.

These colourful mittens are not the only style found in Norway. The fishermen from along the west coast wore felted mittens, often knitted with wool combined with hair, to make the mittens stronger and more hard-wearing. This hair would usually be goat hair, but often horse hair or the hair from the women who themselves were knitting the mittens was incorporated. The mittens were larger than those for normal wear and tied at the wrist with cord. Sometimes they had two thumbs, one on each side of the palm, so that they could be worn on either hand, to even out the wear. Some were patterned, others had initials knitted in, but none were as elaborate as the Selbu mittens.

NORWEGIAN STOCKINGS

The stockings that inspired Marit's mittens were a familiar sight all around Norway. They would be made for everyday wear, as well as being made as special items for confirmations or weddings. In fact, stockings and hats were the most frequently knitted items in many parts of the world, especially the colder countries. These pieces were in great demand, and many women boosted their family income through knitting. They kept notebooks with 'recipes' for knitting, as well as for food, home remedies and wool dyeing. However, for some time, knitting was considered by many to be an unattractive occupation; the way that the needles were held was deemed 'ugly', and it was suggested by one of the characters in Henrik Ibsen's play *A Doll's House* that the more feminine craft of embroidery should be practised. But this view of knitting didn't deter the women who didn't mind how they were portrayed, as long as they could put food on the table for their families, and, however the craft was envisaged, the women of Norway produced some exquisite work. The stockings were usually calf- or knee-length and could be patterned all over with the usual stars, roses or small geometric patterns, such as those shown in the small-dotted-bars charts.

A popular way of making colourful stockings was to knit them with tie-dyed wool. Recipes for dyes would often be printed in what were known as 'household' books or in books of knitting patterns. Chemical dyes were not available until late in the nineteenth century, and most of the stockings were knitted with yarn dyed with woad to make a deep-blue colour. The yarn

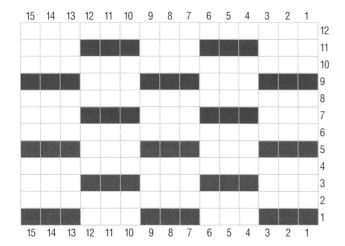

A chart for a small-dotted-bars pattern, as used on fishermen's jerseys. (A swatch worked from this chart is shown in Chapter 4.)

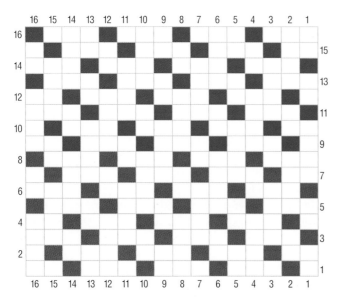

A chart for another variation of the dotted patterns, worked with bands of two colours.

was copied from one of the printed pattern books available at the time. These were the typical stockings of Setesdal, where the famous 'lice' sweaters came from. The men wore plain-white stockings, and the women had black ones, which were dyed after they had been knitted, so that it was easier for the knitter to see the pattern as the stockings were worked. The usual method of construction was to begin at the cuff, shape the calf towards the ankle and then make a heel flap and gusset, as described in Chapter 2, before working the foot and the toe. The toe was usually worked with plain-white yarn. As the stockings became worn, they would sometimes have new foot parts knitted on or an afterthought heel added.

The cabled stockings of Setesdal were more elaborate than those from other areas of Norway and often had their intricate clock designs reaching all the way to the top of the calf. The ribbed parts were usually of twisted knit stitches, making the rib stand out much more and creating a thicker, therefore warmer, fabric than rib worked in the normal way, through the front of the stitch. The cables would cross over only three or four stitches, never being as large as those found on Aran-style stockings.

Knitting was an important part of the school curriculum, and everyone was taught to knit stockings. Several books of instruction were produced in the late nineteenth century, and leaflets were also available, giving the different lengths of each section: cuff, upper leg, calf with its shaping, ankle, heel, foot and toe. Even the depth of the ribbing was given a specific measurement, that is, 'it should be one third of the number of stitches'. All other measurements were based on the number of stitches that were cast on at the beginning; even today, we usually retain this idea in that the number of stitches for the heel should be half the number of stitches at the ankle in width and the number of rounds corresponding to three quarters of the number of heel stitches in length. Look through the stitch dictionary in Chapter 6 and then design yourself a pair of long Norwegian stockings based on these proportions and the number of stitches that you achieve in your swatch.

You might think that, during the winter snows, Norwegians would want to wear thick socks with boots over the top, but, surprisingly, they also had stockings that they wore outdoors with no extra footwear on top. They were more like slipper socks with felted-wool soles. These soles would often be made from worn-out garments and could be replaced as necessary, as they were stitched on to the stocking after it was finished. The uppers were usually worked in plain ribbing, rather than being like the decorated socks and stockings made as gifts, and were often made with shoddy or rag wool.

would be skeined and then tied tightly in various places so that the tied portion would not absorb the dye. Sometimes, the tie-dyed yarn was dried and then tied again in a different position before being dipped into another colour. When stockings were knitted with wool dyed with more than one colour, they were known as *flamme* (flame) stockings.

Other stockings were basically plain ribbed or cabled but were often knitted by using very fine wool and featured a more intricate 'clock' on the outside ankle, similar to the style of the stockings of Austria and Germany; perhaps the clock design

Example of working a stocking

Cast on 54 stitches, and work 18 rounds of your chosen rib (for example, k1, p1 rib or k2, p1 rib). Work the centre stitch (in this case, the 27th stitch or the 28th stitch) as a purl stitch, to mark the 'seam' of the stocking.

Work the top of the calf for 36 rounds (that is, the number of rounds corresponding to two thirds of the cast-on stitch count), then begin shaping the calf by gradually decreasing by 1 stitch on each side of the 'seam' until one quarter of the stitches have been decreased. In this case, it would be 13.5 stitches, so round it up to 14 stitches. That leaves 40 stitches for the rest of the leg. Continue working these 40 stitches for the number of rounds corresponding to one third of the cast-on stitch count, that is, 18 rounds.

Shape the heel on half of the stitches (so, 20 stitches), and make the heel 15 rounds long, corresponding to three quarters of the number of heel stitches.

Turn the heel by knitting two thirds of the heel stitches, which would be 13 or 14 stitches in this case, k2tog and k1, then turn and work back across the section of heel stitches until 6 or 7 stitches are left (the nearest numbers to one third of the number of heel stitches), p2tog, p1.

Repeat these two rows, by working across the central group of stitches in stocking stitch and then working the relevant k2tog, k1 and turn or p2tog, p1 and turn sequence, until all of the unworked stitches are worked off, ending the heel flap by having completed a RS row (if necessary, knit one more row across the heel-flap stitches without decreasing).

Pick up 15 stitches down one side of the heel flap, work across all of the instep stitches, pick up 15 stitches up the other side of the heel flap and then work across all of the heel-flap stitches, to join all of the stocking stitches to be worked in the round again. Shape the gusset on alternate rounds, on each side of the heel-flap stitches, to gradually decrease the stitches at the sides of the heel flap, until the total number of stitches is reduced back to 40. Work the foot to the required length (typically by working the number of rounds corresponding to three quarters of the number of heel stitches), then shape the toe, usually on alternate rounds, until 18 stitches are left, corresponding to one quarter of the number of cast-on stitches.

Fishermen, too, wore these plain, thick socks, but without the sewn-on soles. The men were away from January to April and so needed to take a good supply of warm clothing with them. Most of it would be produced by their wives, who knitted mittens, underwear and jumpers, as well as these coarse, hard-wearing socks. Sometimes they would embroider initials on to the socks, so that each man could identify his own items as they were hung up on the boat to dry, but for the most part these socks were entirely plain.

Other items familiar in Norway, as in the rest of Scandinavia, are knitted hats. The shapes varied a little depending on the area that they came from, but most were decorative and brightly coloured. The hats from Telemark in south-east Norway were shaped like beanies but had a long-pointed top, finished off with a tassel. They were decorated with small border-type patterns, often divided by alternating bands of stripes and spots. Hats from other areas of Norway were decorated with the familiar eight-pointed stars, and such hats were like the ones now machine-made by companies such as Dale of Norway.

DALE OF NORWAY

Until Norway's mills began to spin wool rather than cotton, when the American Civil War halted the USA's export of cotton, almost all of the wool and yarn used for knitting in Norway was handspun. It was not until 1870 that a woollen mill was established in Ålgård in the south-west of Norway, where waterfalls were used to power the mill. However, it was not until the early twentieth century that commercially spun wool became available, from the village of Dale.

In 1879, Peder Jebsen, who had studied textile-production methods in England, set up a factory in the village of Dale near Bergen, in order to produce machine-made garments mainly for export and for sale to the growing tourist industry. His ideal was to produce garments to the highest standard by using only the best wools. His company grew rapidly and has become almost synonymous with Norwegian patterned sweaters. The most famous pattern produced by the company is known as Mariusgenser, and the design is similar to that of the garment belonging to the Knitting and Crochet Guild that was featured earlier in this chapter. As you can see, it is closely related to the *Lusekofte*.

A view of the stars jumper, showing the position of the patterns of the border and yoke.

It was designed by Unn Søiland Dale (1926–2002). She was the design consultant at Sandnes Garn and created this pattern in 1953; it has been popular ever since. Sandnes Uldvarefabrik, the main spinning mill in Norway, estimated that over 5 million copies of the pattern had been sold by 2011. Unn went on to design many more patterns, and she was awarded a gold medal in 2002 for promoting Norwegian hand knitting.

A selection of Dale of Norway booklets.

Dale now produce pattern books of their designs and also make machine-knitted garments for export around the world. Some of the garments are worked in single colours with elaborate cable motifs. I designed a similar jumper for a friend and have included the pattern here. I made it with a locally produced (Norfolk) Southdown wool, but any good-quality aran-weight wool yarn could be used.

ARNE AND CARLOS

Arne Nerjordet and Carlos Zachrison became widely well-known on publication of a book containing patterns for Christmas baubles. All of the designs were inspired by typical Scandinavian motifs and their life in rural Norway and the book became a best-seller throughout the world. They went on to design for various knitting magazines and also international fashion houses such as Comme des Garçons and Urban Outfitters. They are closely associated now with Rowan and Schachenmayr yarns and regularly publish designs for socks and sweaters in the magazines of these companies.

Their work is always very colourful and I have created a Christmas bauble inspired by their first book and one of the typical Scandinavian border patterns.

CHRISTMAS BAUBLE

Materials

Scraps of 4ply in four colours
Set of 5, size 2.75mm double-pointed needles
Polyester stuffing

With two of the double-pointed needles and Pink, cast on 4 sts. Following the chart for the placing of the design, work increases/decreases as follows:

1st round: *Kfb. Rep from * around. 8 sts.
Divide sts onto 4 needles. Join into a round: taking care not to twist stitches.
Place marker at first st.
2nd round: K8.
3rd round: *Kfb. Rep from * around. (16sts)
4th round: K16.
5th round: *K1. M1. K2. M1. K1. Rep from * around. (24sts)
6th round: K24.
7th round: *K1. M1. K4. M1. K1. Rep from * around. (32sts)
8th round: K32.
9th round: *K1. M1. K6. M1. K1. Rep from * around. (40sts)
10th round: K40.
11th round: *K1. M1. K8. M1. K1. Rep from * around. (48sts)
12th round: K48.
13th round: *K1. M1. K10. M1. K1. Rep from * around. (56sts)
14th to 23rd rounds: K56.
24th round: *K2tog. K10. ssk. Rep from * around. (48sts)
25th round: K48.
26th round: *K2tog. K8. ssk. Rep from * around. (40sts)
27th round: K40.
28th round: *K2tog. K6. ssk. Rep from * around. (32sts)
29th round: K32.
30th round: *K2tog. K4. ssk. Rep from * around. (24sts)
31st round: K24.
32nd round: *K2tog. K2. ssk. Rep from * around. (16sts)
33rd round: K16.
34th round: *K2tog. ssk. Rep from * around. (8sts)
35th round: K8. Break yarn, leaving a long end.
Thread this end through the stitches but do not fasten it off yet.

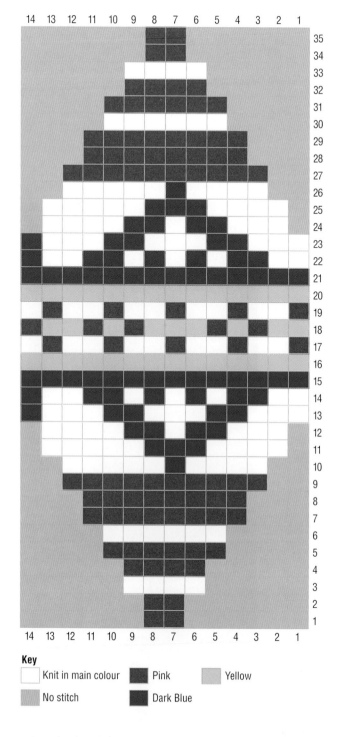

Key

☐ Knit in main colour	■ Pink	☐ Yellow
☐ No stitch	■ Dark Blue	

A chart for the Christmas bauble design.

Block the ball carefully then, when it is dry, fill it with polyester stuffing until it is quite firm.
Fasten off the 8 stitches securely. Fold the yarn in half and twist it tightly; fold it in half again to form a hanging loop and fasten it to the top of the bauble.

CHRISTMAS SWEATER

Another item that has now become a familiar sight at Christmas time is the 'Christmas Sweater'! These garments often use traditional Norwegian motifs such as reindeer, snowflakes, pine trees, etc., usually in bright and often gaudy colours. Using one of the schematics from Chapter 7, work this chart, or adapt it to use some of the other motifs from Chapter 6. If the number of stitches in the chart won't fit exactly into your chosen size, place it as a central panel and work the remaining stitches in a textured stitch or plain stocking stitch.

Key

- RS: knit / WS: purl
- Blue
- Black
- Green
- Red

A chart for a Christmas sweater design.

CABLED JUMPER

Size

To fit a chest circumference of 42in

Materials

800g of aran-weight yarn

Needles

1 pair 5mm needles
Circular 4mm needle

Tension

24sts and 24 rows to 10cm/4in using 5mm needles
over diamond-cable patt

Abbreviations

2/2 LC = slip next 2 stitches to cable needle, place
cable needle at front of work, k2 and then k2 from
cable needle.
2/2 LPC = slip next 2 stitches to cable needle, place
cable needle at front of work, p2 and then k2 from
cable needle.
2/2 RC = slip next 2 stitches to cable needle, place
cable needle at back of work, k2 and then k2 from
cable needle.
2/2 RPC = slip next 2 stitches to cable needle, place
cable needle at back of work, k2 and then p2 from
cable needle.

Diamond-cable written instructions

Row 1 (RS): K10, *(k4, p2, k2, p2) × 2, k10. Work from * 4
times in total, k4. (134sts)
Row 2 (WS): K4, *p2, k2, p2, k6, p2, k2, p4, k2, p2, k6.
Work from * 4 times in total, p2, k2, p2, k4.
Row 3: K10, *k4, p2, k2, p2, 2/2 LC, p2, k2, p2, k10. Work
from * 4 times in total, k4.
Row 4: Rep row 2.
Rows 5–8: Rep rows 1–4.
Row 9: K10, *k4, p2, k2, 2/2 RPC, 2/2 LPC, k2, p2, k10;
work from * 4 times in total, k4.
Row 10: K4, *p2, k2, p2, k6, p4, k4, p4, k6; work from * 4
times in total, p2, k2, p2, k4.
Row 11: K10, *k4, p2, 2/2 RC, p4, 2/2 LC, p2, k10; work
from * 4 times in total, k4.
Row 12: Rep row 10.
Row 13: K10, *k4, (2/2 RPC, 2/2 LPC) × 2, k10; work from *
4 times in total, k4.

A swatch for the Dale-of-Norway-inspired cabled jumper.

Row 14: K4, *p2, k2, (p2, k4) × 2, p4, k4, p2, k4; work from
* 4 times in total, p2, k2, p2, k4.
Row 15: K10, *k2, 2/2 RC, (p4, 2/2 LC) × 2, k8; work from *
4 times in total, k4.
Row 16: K4, *(p2, k2) × 2, (p4, k4) × 2, p4, k2; work from *
4 times in total, p2, k2, p2, k4.
Row 17: K10, *k4, (2/2 LPC, 2/2 RPC) × 2, k10; work from *
4 times in total, k4.
Row 18: K4, *(p2, k2) × 3, p4, k4, p4, k2, p2, k2; work from
* 4 times in total, p2, k2, p2, k4.
Row 19: K10, *k4, p2, 2/2 RC, p4, 2/2 RC, p2, k10; work
from * 4 times in total, k4.
Row 20: Rep row 18.
Row 21: K10, *k4, 2/2 RC, 2/2 LPC, 2/2 RPC, 2/2 LC, k10;
work from * 4 times in total, k4.
Row 22: Rep row 16.
Row 23: K10, *k2, (2/2 LC, p4) × 2, 2/2 RC, k8; work from *
4 times in total, k4.
Row 24: Rep row 14.
Row 25: Rep row 17.
Row 26: Rep row 10.
Row 27: K10, *k4, p2, 2/2 LC, p4, 2/2 RC, p2, k10; work
from * 4 times in total, k4.
Row 28: Rep row 10.
Row 29: K10, *k4, p2, k2, 2/2 LPC, 2/2 RPC, k2, p2, k10;
work from * 4 times in total, k4.
Row 30: Rep row 2.
Row 31: Rep row 1.
Row 32: Rep row 2.
Row 33: Rep row 3.
Row 34: Rep row 2.

Back

Cast on 134sts with 5mm needles, and work diamond-cable patt by following the accompanying chart or written instructions until piece measures 12in (about 72 rows) from cast-on edge, ending with RS facing, having completed a WS row.
Mark current row at both ends for armholes.
Work as set for 10in more (about 60 rows). Place all sts on to a holder.

Front

Work as for the back until piece measures 12in.
Mark current row at both ends for armholes. Work 6 rows, ending with RS facing, having completed a WS row.

Neck shaping

Patt 44sts (for left front), cast off next 46sts, patt rem 44sts (for right front). Cont working on set of 44sts for right front in patt until piece measures same as for back.
Slip these sts to a holder.
Return to rem 44sts for left front, and work left front as for right front. Leave these sts on a holder.

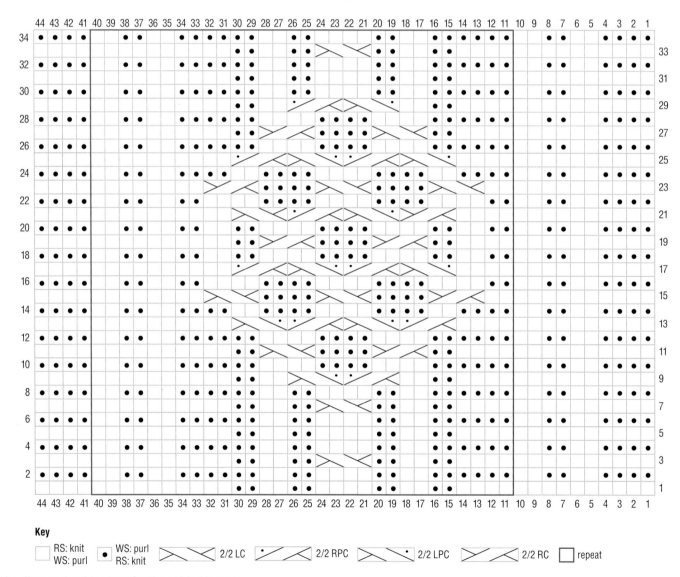

The diamond-cable chart for the cabled jumper.

Sleeves

Cast on 44sts with 5mm needles. Work in diamond-cable pattern, and, at the same time, inc by 1 stitch at each end of every alt row 20 times (84sts) and then every 3rd row 16 times (116sts).
Work even in patt until piece measures 15in from cast-on edge. Cast off loosely.

Work second sleeve as for first sleeve.

Shoulder seaming

Work Kitchener stitch or three-needle cast-offs to join left front and right front to back; form these shoulder seams by using all of the stitches on the holders for left front and right front and the outermost 44sts of stitches on holder for back.

Collar

Using 4mm needles, with RS facing, pick up and knit the 23sts of the left side of the front cast-off, then turn the work. Work in k2, p2 rib across 22sts and then k1. Work in rib as set until collar rib reaches to the level of the shoulder seam. Slip these sts on to a holder.
Again using 4mm needles and with RS facing, pick up and knit the 23sts of the right side of the front cast-off, then turn the work. K1, then work in k2, p2 rib across rem 22sts. Work in rib as set for the same number of rows as worked for the first side of the collar (that is, until collar rib reaches to the level of the shoulder seam).
Next row: With RS facing, work in rib as set across the 23sts of the right side of the collar, the 46sts rem on holder for back neck and then the 23sts rem on holder for the left side of the collar. Work 2in of rib as set across all 92sts. Change to using 5mm needles, and work 2in more of rib as set. Cast off loosely in patt.

Finishing

Sew cast-off edges of sleeves to separate armhole edges, easing in the top of each sleeve to fit and using the marked rows of the back and front pieces to establish the depth and locations of the underarms.

The Dale of Norway jumper that was the inspiration for this cabled sweater.

Sew both side seams and sleeve seams. Sew together the adjacent vertical edges of the left front and left side of the collar and of the right front and right side of the collar, by using mattress stitch or whip stitch.
Weave in all yarn ends.

This type of textured knitwear is actually less familiar in Norway, and most of the textiles are multicoloured, along the lines of the colours and styles of folk costumes, with designs probably having been taken from weaving and embroidery.

HEN KNITTING

A movement began in Norway in the 1970s that objected to these 'traditional' designs, the followers of which felt that these designs were restrictive and suppressed creativity. The movement was started by Kirsten Hofstätter, a Danish knitter and author, and become known as hen knitting.

At that time, it was not possible to buy yarn without buying the pattern to go with it. Kirsten objected to this and encouraged knitters to create their own designs and use non-traditional colours, in fact, using colours that, conventionally, would not be thought to go well together. There is no reason why we cannot do this today, following the dictum of Igor Stravinsky and letting individual knitting experiences inform the present. There are many ways that the charts in Chapter 6 can be worked in ways that retain the Scandinavian feel but appear more modern. However, there is still a place for traditional knitting and colourwork, and textured knits are still more familiar in Sweden and Denmark, as we shall see in subsequent chapters.

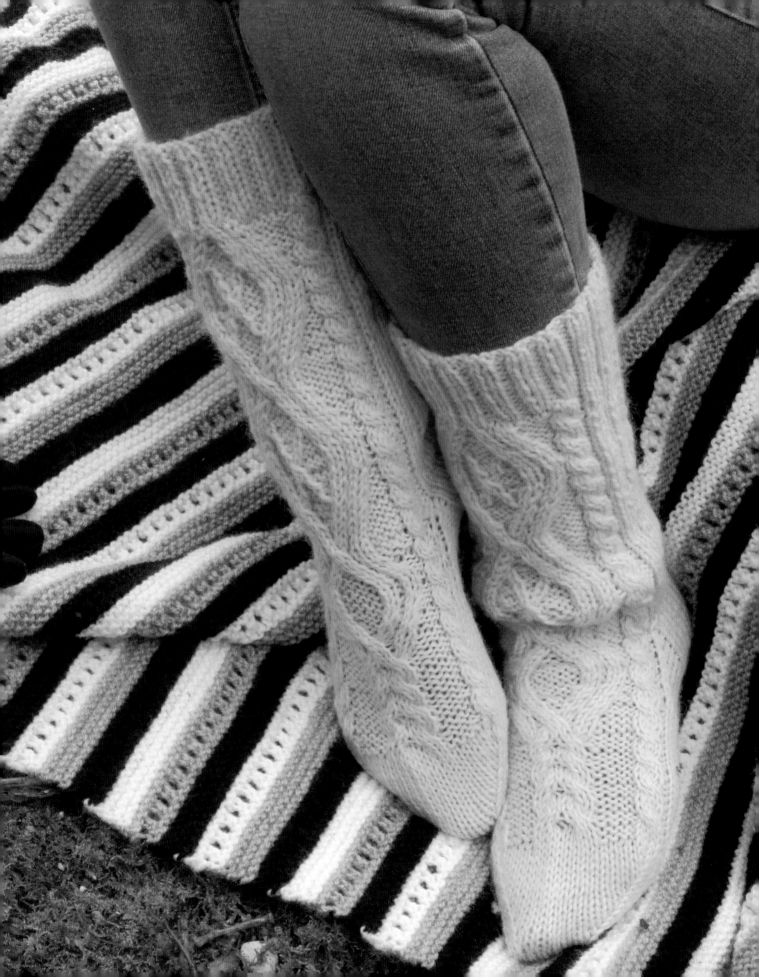

CHAPTER 4

SWEDEN

SOME HISTORY

As in the other Scandinavian countries, the technique of *naalbinding* was used before knitting was 'discovered', to produce items made from the wool of the local sheep. It is a slow and laborious technique, where the yarn is threaded through the eye of a sewing needle and then worked in the round through a series of loops, as described in Chapter 2, and it is more akin to tatting. It was mainly used for making mittens, socks and leggings of various kinds; the socks were of two main types: 'ordinary' socks, to be worn inside shoes, and sturdier, thicker socks, to be worn over the top of snow-shoes. Then, in the mid-seventeenth century, a new governor of Halland, one of the districts of southern Sweden, was appointed. He brought with him his Dutch wife, Magna Brita Cracau. Hand knitting was already well-established in Europe, and the Dutch were particularly skilled at the craft. The Victoria and Albert Museum holds an extraordinary petticoat measuring over 3 metres around and decorated all over with birds, animals and flowers, picked out in purl stitches on a knitted background. It is dated to c.1700–1750, showing that knitting must already have been a well-known craft to have reached this level of skilled workmanship. Magna encouraged the people of Halland to form groups, or 'bingegillen', where they could practise their newly learned skills and encourage one another. 'Att binga' is an old dialect term from the Halland region, meaning 'to knit'. The knitted items produced by these groups were soon being sent to other parts of Scandinavia, and more knitting groups were set up elsewhere. From various national records and inventories that contain references to a person's occupation, it can be seen that many people supported themselves through the practice of knitting gloves and stockings. The items were relatively simple and quickly produced, with the Swedish Army being the largest market for the Halland stockings.

However, the nineteenth century brought industrialization and, just as had happened in Britain and other parts of Europe, the demand for hand-knitted goods fell dramatically. To help those who had now lost their income from knitting, Swedish Handcraft was founded in 1899, with the aim of preserving the traditional crafts. Other groups were set up locally, including the Halland Knitting Craft Association (*Hallandska Bindslojdsforeningen*) set up by Berta Borgström, the wife of the doctor of Laholm. She obtained yarn from the British company Patons, because it was softer but more firmly spun than yarn made of Swedish wool. To promote the products, Berta designed a label with a Bjarbo motif, similar to that of the Scottish thistle that is often used on Fair Isle garments. The motif was worked in red and blue on a white or cream background. This design was usually worked all over a garment in full or adapted as a border feature. Surprisingly for such a complex design, it was often knitted by two knitters

A swatch of the Bjarbo motif that is used for the slouchy hat in Chapter 7.

A motif featuring a snowflake with ferns.

at once, working on the same garment. This is not as difficult as it seems when the work is done on four or more double-pointed needles. One knitter would sit facing the other and work on their half of the body and then the work would be passed around for them to work on the other half!

To ensure that the items knitted by the *Hallandska Bindslojdsforeningen* could be identified, and their quality maintained, the items all bore the label with a small version of the Bjarbo motif that Berta had designed. The work became more and more popular, especially with people involved in various winter sports, and eventually the group moved into their own premises. Pieces were exported to the USA, and members of the royal families of Sweden and Denmark bought jackets, hats and mittens from them. Unlike the traditional rectangular, tubular knitted items, many of these Binge knitwear items were shaped and could be customized for the person ordering it. The group even produced lengths of knitting that could be cut and fashioned by the buyer into whatever style they chose.

The association is still in existence but now seems to concentrate more on selling wool and patterns in order for people to knit their own items.

There are several instances of similarities between Scottish and Scandinavian patterns, just as there are between their languages. It is difficult to know the precise origin of these various motifs, many of which are seen in fabrics from other areas of the world. Is it to do with the geometric shapes of stitches, or is it the interaction between travellers, especially

on the trade routes? While we look for inspiration now from thousands of miles away via the internet, on the hunt for novel ideas, knitters then had to rely on chance meetings. Or perhaps their inspiration came from the places, plants and animals around the knitters, in the same way that our surroundings can be inspiration for us today. There are many instances of trees and flowers being used as decoration; for example, the Norwegian star was often given a more rounded shape to resemble a stylized flower, as in the centre of the featured motif.

Another familiar motif seen in Swedish designs is that of a row of people, as seen in the featured pattern for a hat. I have also given charts for an owl and a tree, as these, too, were frequently used in Sweden, where knitters often used elements of the natural world as inspiration for their designs. For additional charts featuring fauna and flora, see Chapter 6.

LITTLE-MAIDS HAT

A close-up of the little-maids hat.

Size

To fit an average adult head of about 20in in circumference

Materials

1 × 50g ball of DK-weight yarn in each of three colours (MC, CC1, CC2)

Needles

5 double-pointed 3.25mm needles (or an equivalent circular needle, if preferred)
5 double-pointed 3.75mm needles (or an equivalent circular needle, if preferred)

Tension

22sts and 30 rows to 10cm/4in using 3.75mm needles over colourwork patt

This hat is worked in the round from the bottom up, beg with a ribbed hem.

Using 3.25mm needles and CC1, cast on 110sts, and join to work in the round. Work 2in of k1, p1 rib, and, at the same time, inc evenly to 112sts on last round.

Change to 3.75mm needles, and work 4 rounds with CC2. Work 1 round with MC.

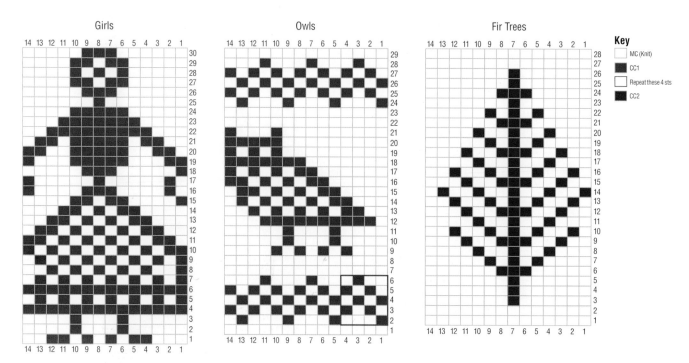

A selection of charts that can be used for the little-maids hat.

Now, work your chosen chart with MC and CC1.

Next, with MC, (k11, k3tog) around. (96sts)

With CC2, knit 3 rounds, then (k9, k3tog) around. (80sts)

With CC1, (k7, k3tog) around (64sts), knit 1 round, then (k5, k3tog) around (48sts).

Cont with CC1, dec as established on every round until 8sts rem.

Leaving a tail, cut the yarn, thread the yarn through the rem sts, draw up sts, to close the hole at the top of the hat, and fasten off firmly.

Weave in all yarn ends.

A typical Scandinavian outfit, including a hat and patterned sweater.

SWEATERS

While the basic shapes of the garments were more or less the same, knitted in the round and with sleeves knitted from the cuff up and sewn in after the pieces of a garment's body had been completed, some were only short and worn under a bibbed dungaree-type garment. Knitters of the Hälsingland region of Sweden developed these sweaters with all-over patterns. A motif was usually worked as two halves, with colour dividing the motif. For example, a frequently used pattern in the Delsbo region would begin with red on black and then change halfway through to green on black, making it look as though there were more than one motif present.

The knitters of Halland province on the south-west coast of Sweden made sweaters for the local fishermen in the same basic tube shape that was popular in the nineteenth century. These sweaters were often two-coloured but knitted tightly with all-over patterns of diamonds or other geometric shapes. In the centre of the front there would be a small rectangle containing a date and/or the wearer's initials. The sweaters would often have saddle shoulders worked with a different, larger pattern and the same motif, or a similar one, on the cuffs.

The shape of these fishermen's sweaters is replicated in this design for a small child's sweater. There is very little shaping, so the large motifs won't be disturbed by curving of the armholes, and working of the motif is finished before the neck shaping is begun. All of these aspects are approaches that would make knitting the items much quicker – a positive thing when almost everything had to be made by hand and when such knitting was frequently done to add to the family income.

A swatch of a small-dotted-bars pattern that has been used on fishermen's jerseys.

CHILD'S T-SHAPED SWEATER

Size

To fit a chest circumference of 22 (24, 26, 28)in
Actual measurements: chest circumference 21½ (25¾, 28, 30)in; back length 14 (15, 16½, 18)in; sleeve-seam length 8½ (10½, 12, 13½)in

Materials

150 (200, 200, 250)g of DK-weight yarn in MC
50 (50, 100, 100)g of DK-weight yarn in CC

Needles

1 pair 3.5mm needles
1 pair 4mm needles
Circular 3.5mm needle

Tension

22sts and 28 rows to 10cm/4in using 4mm needles over st. st

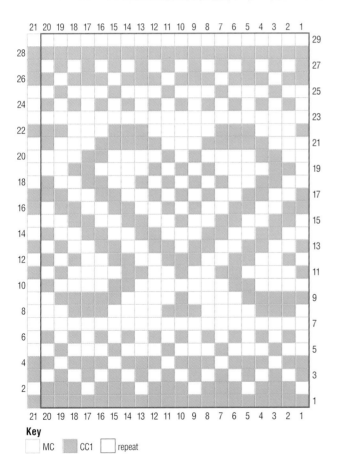

Key

MC | CC1 | repeat

The hearts chart for the child's T-shaped sweater.

Scandinavian knitting was frequently done in the round, but it could also be worked by more than one person and the children of the family would often knit for themselves or their brothers and sisters, each one of them working a separate piece. It would not be difficult to adapt it to knit in the round, picking up the stitches for the sleeves and knitting them downwards.

Back

Using 3.5mm needles and MC, cast on 61 (73, 79, 85)sts. Work k1, p1 rib until piece measures 2in from cast-on edge. Change to 4mm needles, and work rows 1–6 of hearts chart. Work 3 (3, 4, 4)in more of st. st with MC only.
Now, work the whole hearts chart (rows 1–29), starting at stitch 1 for the 1st size, stitch 7 for the 2nd size, stitch 20 for the 3rd size and stitch 3 for the 4th size; at the same time, when piece measures 6 (7, 8, 9)in from cast-on edge, mark the current row at both ends for the underarms.
Work 5½ (6, 6½, 7)in more in st. st with MC.

Shoulder shaping

Cast off 8 (10, 12, 13)sts at beg of next 2 rows and 8 (11, 12, 14)sts at beg of following 2 rows. Slip rem 29 (31, 31, 31)sts on to holder for back neck.

Front

Work as for back until piece measures 2 (2½, 2½, 3)in less than back, remembering to mark position of underarms as previously.

Neck shaping

Work 23 (29, 32, 35)sts in st. st with MC (for left front). Slip the next 15sts to a holder for front neck. With a second ball of yarn, work rem 23 (29, 32, 35)sts (for right front). Cont working on set of 23sts for right front in st. st, and, at the same time, dec by 1 stitch at neck edge every row 7 times, until 16sts rem.
Work even until armhole measures same as for back.

Shoulder shaping

Cast off 8 (10, 12, 13)sts at beg of next row and 8 (11, 12, 14)sts at beg of following alt row.

Return to rem 23 (29, 32, 35)sts for left front, and work left front as for right front.

Sleeves

Using 3.5mm needles and MC, cast on 35 (37, 38, 40)sts. Work k1, p1 rib until piece measures 1½ (1¾, 2, 2)in from cast-on edge, ending with RS facing, having completed a WS row.

Next row: Knit across row, and, at the same time, inc evenly to 41 (41, 42, 44)sts.

Change to 4mm needles, and purl across row.

Work rows 1–6 of hearts chart.

Cont in st. st with MC, and, at the same time, inc by 1 stitch at each end of every 4th row 2 (3, 10, 10) times and then every 5th row 8 (10, 6, 8) times, until there are 61 (67, 74, 80)sts.

Work even in st. st until piece measures 8½ (10½, 12, 13½) in from cast-on edge.

Cast off loosely.

Work second sleeve as for first sleeve.

Sew left front to back to form left shoulder seam.

The child's T-shaped sweater, with a band of hearts around the body.

With RS facing, using a circular 3.5mm needle and MC, knit
29 (32, 31, 31)sts from back-neck holder, pick up and knit
15 (17, 17, 18)sts along left-front neck edge, knit 15sts from
front-neck holder and pick up and knit 15 (17, 17, 18)sts
along the right-front neck edge. [74 (80, 80, 82)sts]
Work 8 rows of k1, p1 rib.
Cast off loosely in patt.

Finishing

Sew right front to back to form right shoulder seam, and sew
neck seam with mattress stitch or whip stitch. Sew cast-off edges
of sleeves to separate armhole edges, easing in top of each sleeve
to fit and using the marked rows of the back and front pieces to
establish the depth and locations of the underarms. Sew both
side seams and sleeve seams, and weave in all yarn ends.

MITTENS

Hats and fishermen's sweaters were not the only items
knitted in Sweden; as for the other countries of Scandinavia, they also had mittens. They were usually knitted with
black and white yarns and then overdyed with madder to
produce a deep-red colour. Some of the mittens would
have motifs knitted in white cotton which, as they were
knitted so tightly, did not always take the dye completely,
and bits of the white fibres can still be seen on some pairs
of mittens held in the Nordic Museum (*Nordiska museet*).
If the mittens were knitted for special occasions, they
would have the initials of the recipient and relevant date
incorporated into the pattern bands, with the main part
of the hand being knitted in a dotted pattern like the 'lice'
pattern of Norway.

In the northernmost part of Sweden, a group of
nomadic people called Sami have developed their own
style of mittens. These mittens don't have ribbed cuffs
but, instead, a braid-like cast-on similar to that used in
two-end, or twined, knitting. Another similarity is the use
of the twisted purl stitch to divide the bands of motifs.
The hand is decorated in bright colours, sometimes with
more than two colours in a row. The patterns are almost
eastern in appearance, perhaps because of the closeness to
Russia. Each mitten is shaped at the top by working sets of

A typical pair of Swedish colourwork mittens.

decreases more like those at the top of a beanie, or the toe
of a sock, giving a more rounded shape than the triangular
top of a Norwegian mitten. As with many of the older-style
mittens, the thumb is added as an afterthought, sometimes
being referred to as a peasant thumb. Another unusual
feature of the Sami mittens is the twisted cord, sometimes
with a tassel, at the cuff edge of each mitten. It is thought
that this cord was to tie the two mittens together so that
they could be hung up to dry.

TEXTURED KNITTING

As well as the colourwork that we associate with the Scandinavian countries, there are also the single-colour techniques
worked by making purl stitches on a knit background, sometimes known as 'damask work'. Damask fabric is woven, usually
with a dull background and a glossy, shinier fibre being used to
produce a pattern of leaves, flowers, birds or animals. The term
is used in knitting to describe the fabric produced by working
the background with smooth knit stitches and the motifs with
purl stitches that stand slightly proud of the background.

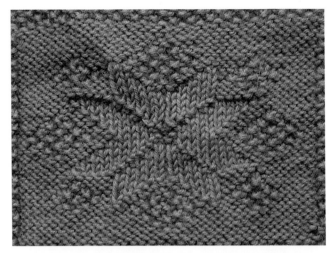

A swatch of the star-with-small-diamonds motif. (The chart for this pattern can be found in Chapter 6.)

A swatch of the star-with-diamonds motif.

Damask work

As alluded to earlier, this technique was probably brought to Sweden by Magna Brita Cracau, the wife of the governor of Halland, who knew it from her home in the Netherlands. It was most often used on waistcoats. The patterns may have been copied from those on the Danish nightshirts, but there are also examples of seventeenth-century stockings that have clocks worked in these textured patterns along the side of the legs, in imitation of the embroidered motifs on cloth stockings.

The waistcoats that were knitted by using this type of textured work were usually made with naturally coloured wool and then dyed. Some of the motifs are variations on

the star or snowflake; others are quite elaborate, representing flowers and foliage, such as the featured design of a carnation.

This small design could be worked all over or used as a motif on a glove or sock.

If you prefer to follow written instructions rather than a chart, they are as follows:

Row 1 (RS): K6, p3, k12. (21sts)
Row 2 (WS): P11, k1, p3, k1, p5.
Row 3: K5, (p1, k1) × 2, p1, k11.
Row 4: P5, k2, p4, k1, p1, k2, p2, k3, p1.
Row 5: P2, k6, p1, k1, p1, k2, p4, k4.
Row 6: P4, k4, p2, k1, p1, k1, p5, k3.
Row 7: K1, p5, k1, p1, k3, p1, k2, p2, k1, p2, k2.
Row 8: P1, k4, p2, k3, p4, k4, p3.
Row 9: K1, p5, k5, p1, k4, p4, k1.
Row 10: P2, k2, p1, k2, p3, k1, p7, k3.
Row 11: P2, k8, p1, k2, p4, k4.
Row 12: P4, k4, p3, k1, p5, k3, p1.
Row 13: K9, p1, k4, p2, k5.
Row 14: P10, k3, p8.
Row 15: K8, p3, k10.
Row 16: P5, (k3, p2) × 2, k3, p3.
Row 17: K2, p5, k1, p3, k1, p5, k4.
Row 18: P5, k4, p1, k3, p1, k4, p3.
Row 19: K4, p2, k2, p3, k2, p2, k6.
Row 20: P10, k1, p1, k1, p8.
Row 21: K2, p1, (k1, p1, k1, p2) × 2, (k1, p1) × 2, k4.
Row 22: P5, (k1, p1) × 6, k1, p3.
Row 23: K4, (p1, k1) × 5, p1, k6.
Row 24: P7, (k1, p1) × 4, k1, p5.
Row 25: K6, (p1, k1) × 3, p1, k8.
Row 26: P9, k1, p3, k1, p7.
Row 27: Knit.
Row 28: Purl.
Rows 29–30: Rep rows 27–28.

Twined knitting

Another way of producing a warm, textured fabric that was used was by twining two strands of yarn together, often being knitted from the inside and outside of the same ball of yarn. This creates a fabric that is thick and warm but not as flexible as damask knitting or single-stranded knitting.

In 1974, an archaeological team found an old glove under the slag heap of what was once a thriving copper mine at Falun.

A damask-work textured pattern representing a carnation.

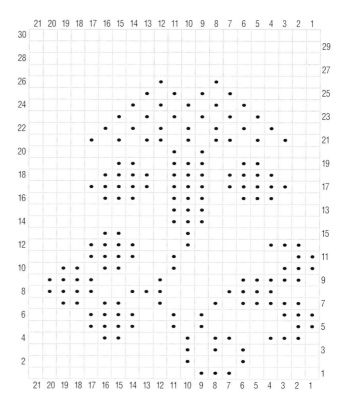

The chart for the textured carnation motif.

The date of the last use of the slag heap was already known to be around 1680, so this proved that the glove dated from that time at the latest, and it is the oldest piece of knitting yet found in Sweden. The glove was made by using the technique with the Swedish name of '*tvåändsstickning*', which makes a fabric that has a double layer of yarn, for extra warmth.

If one ball is to be used for twined knitting, it has to be wound so that the yarn strands can be drawn from both the centre and the outside of the ball. This causes the strands to twist around themselves, and, gradually, the build up of twist becomes unmanageable and the stands are impossible to work with. To remedy this, the ball is suspended by holding up the knitting, so that the overly twisted yarn connecting the held-up knitting to the suspended ball will gradually untwist. Sticking a pencil or a knitting needle through the ball stops it from unravelling as it spins around.

Techniques

The first thing to note is that this is going to be a slow way of working! Don't try to hold the yarn in your normal way, especially if you are a continental-style knitter who holds the working yarn for it to be picked up from the left index finger. For twined or two-end knitting, both ends of the yarn are held on one hand, and the yarn is always thrown (as in English-style

Woollen versus worsted

There are two ways of constructing a yarn for knitting; the resulting yarns are known as woollen-spun and worsted-spun. Woollen-spun yarns are light and airy, as well as being a little bit hairy! Because they are not spun tightly, the fibres and strands of the yarn can rub and break easily. Worsted-spun yarns are firmer, denser and stronger. However, because worsted yarn is denser than woollen yarn, it has fewer metres per gram, and so more grams of worsted-spun yarn than woollen-spun yarn are required to make the same garment. Worsted-spun yarns are spun more tightly, with extra twist, which makes them smoother, firmer and more lustrous. The fibres for woollen-spun yarns, on the other hand, are carded back and forth, which makes the fibres lie in all directions. They are spun lightly to preserve the bounciness and elasticity of the fibres, and these characteristics are transferred to the resulting yarn. As a result, woollen-spun yarns look plumper and feel lighter than worsted-spun yarns.

knitting) rather than picked (as in continental-style knitting). The second thing to note is that there are no floats along the back of the work, and it is not stranded in the way that Fair Isle is. While two colours can be used, this technique is more often worked with one colour, by using two ends of the same ball of yarn. The patterns are mainly textured rather than coloured. However, a second colour is often used as a feature in the cast-on row, so I have designed the featured wristlets to be started with two colours of yarn.

There are two ways to start, as presented in the following sections.

Method 1

Make a slip knot with the contrast-colour yarn, leaving a tail of about three times the intended length of the finished width of the knitting, and place the slip knot on the needle. Make a slip knot with the main-colour yarn, leaving only a short tail (to later be woven in), and place this slip knot on to the needle, next to the contrast-colour slip knot. Hold the contrast-colour yarn in the left hand, and carry the yarn tail over the thumb. Insert the needle into the loop made over the thumb, and knit a stitch with the main-colour yarn, by pulling it through the thumb loop. Continue in this way, knitting stitches with the main-colour yarn through loops of the contrast-colour yarn, for the required number of stitches to be cast on (excluding the contrast-colour slip knot). This contrast-colour slip knot will be undone when you finish the piece and, therefore, does not count as a stitch.

Method 2

The wrong side of a swatch of twined knitting including decorative stitches.

Make a slip knot with all three strands of yarn, leaving a contrast-colour tail of about three times the length of the finished width of the knitting, and place the slip knot on to the needle. Proceed as for cast-on method 1, and work alternately with one end of the main-colour yarn and then the other one, twisting the yarns over each other in the same direction every time that you change ends, until the required number of stitches have been cast on (excluding the three-strand slip knot). This slip knot will be undone when you finish the piece and, therefore, does not count as a stitch.

Both of these methods give a row of contrast-colour stitches that look as though they are woven into the main-colour stitches.

The stitches of subsequent rounds are knitted with alternate ends of the main colour, by twisting the second end over the first before knitting the second stitch and then the first one over the second for the next stitch, and so on. Repeat to the end of the round, always alternating the ends and twisting them in the same direction throughout, for example, by taking the second one over the top of the first.

Twined knitting is usually worked in the round, as the working the motifs is slightly easier this way. If you do want to work twined knitting flat then the purled side is worked in a similar way, but the strands are carried underneath each other so that they slope in the same direction as when they

This swatch includes several twined-3 (or hook or crook) stitches: near the centre of the swatch is a single twined-3 stitch, above which are two other single twined-3 stitches and below which is a chain of twined-3 stitches.

Most knitting yarns are spun with a Z-twist, that is, twisted to the right, and plied with an S-twist, twisted to the left. The yarns spun in Sweden for twined knitting were traditionally spun with an S-twist and plied with a Z-twist. The process of knitting automatically adds a twist to the yarn that gradually untwists a Z-plied yarn (a yarn plied with a Z-twist), making it softer and more open, as required for a warm fabric that traps the air and insulates the body.

are worked on the knitted side of the fabric.

Twined-knitting stitches create a smooth surface on the front of the work. The right side of the fabric looks like stocking stitch, but, if you turn it over to the back, you will see a series of sloped stitches rather than the ridges that you get with single-stranded knitting.

Purl stitches can also be created on the right side of the fabric as a decorative feature, making what looks like a braid. The purl stitches are worked in the same way as the knit stitches, taking one strand over the other before working each stitch. This gives a ridge of sloping stitches on the right side and is often worked in two colours to emphasize this characteristic.

Another way to make a motif is to work a twined-3 stitch (also called a hook stitch or crook stitch), where the stitches that form the pattern are purled but one strand of yarn is kept to the front while the other strand is used to work the following stitch as a knit stitch. The third stitch is also purled and then the just-used yarn at the front of the work is taken to the back.

To form one twined-3 stitch, knit with alternate strands as far as the first stitch of the motif, bring the next yarn strand to be worked with to the front (leaving the other yarn strand at the back of the work), and purl the stitch with the yarn strand at the front in the normal way. Leave this strand of yarn at the front, and knit the next stitch with the yarn at the back. Purl the following stitch with the yarn still at the front, then take this yarn to the back, and knit the rest of the row by using the two strands alternately.

A series of these groups of three stitches makes what is called a chain path. The groups of three stitches can be used to form a motif such as a cross, zigzag or diamond. In the pattern for the wristlets, I have given a chart for a cross motif, but it would not be difficult to change this to a motif of your own design.

Finishing

Swedish mittens, especially those knitted with twined knitting, are often finished with a long cord. The method of making this is to take four ends of yarn, two of each colour. Tie them together at the top, then hold two in each hand side by side, keeping them spaced. Pass the right strand in the right hand behind the others and between the two on the left hand, bring it forwards and over the right strand on the left hand. Pass the left strand on the left hand behind the others and over the left strand of the right hand in the same way and continue working these two movements until the braid is completed. Either tie a knot at the end or fasten the strands back into the braid.

TWINED-KNITTING WRISTLETS

Size
To fit average adult wrists

Materials
50g of Fibreworks Norfolk Horn yarn in MC
25g of Fibreworks Norfolk Horn yarn in CC

Needles
Circular 3.5mm needle (or an equivalent set of double-pointed needles)

Tension
28sts and 26 rows to 10cm/4in using 3.5mm needles over twined-knitting st. st

I have adapted the typical twined-knitting cast-on to require just two strands, to make it a bit less awkward to perform. It may be that this was the most popular way of casting on anyway, rather than using three yarn strands in total and twisting the two strands of the main colour after casting on each stitch.

Worked from the top of the hand to the cuff, with the twined-knitting technique being used throughout.
Make a slip knot with 1 strand of MC and 1 strand of CC.
Cast on 56sts by using the long-tail cast-on with CC as the yarn running around the thumb.
Break off CC (or, instead, loosely carry the CC yarn up on the WS of the fabric until needed), and join in a second strand of MC.

Rounds 1–3: Work twined-knitting knit stitches around.
Round 4: K1, join in a strand of CC, *bring CC to front, p1 with CC, k1 with MC, p1 with CC, take CC to back, k1 with MC; rep from * to end. Break off CC.
Round 5: Work twined-knitting knit stitches around with MC.
Round 6: K2, join in a strand of CC; work as for round 4 from *.
Rounds 7–9: Work twined-knitting knit stitches around with MC.
Round 10: Work twined-knitting purl stitches around by alternating MC and CC.

A close-up of the twined-knitting wristlets, showing the two-colour cast-ons (at the tops of the wristlets), borders and cast-offs (at the bottoms of the cuffs of the wristlets) and the cross motifs.

Tip

If the yarns are twisted under one another, the ridge will slope to the right; if they are twisted over each, other it will slope to the left.

Rounds 11–14: Work twined-knitting knit stitches around with MC.
Round 15: With MC, k10, work the next 13sts by following round 1 of the twined-knitting cross chart, k33.
Rounds 16–23: With MC, k10, work the next 13sts by following the next round of the twined-knitting cross chart, k33.
Rounds 24–28: Work twined-knitting knit stitches around with MC.
Round 29: Work as for round 10.
Rounds 30–32: Work twined-knitting knit stitches around with MC.
Cast off by working alternately with MC and CC.
Weave in all yarn ends.

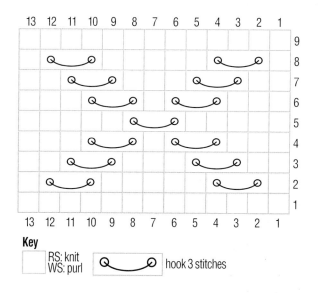

Key

RS: knit WS: purl	hook 3 stitches

The twined-knitting cross chart.

CABLED KNITTING

Travelling stitches

The featured stockings are in the Norsk Folkemuseum in Norway, but similar cabled stockings are still found throughout Scandinavia and became very popular as ski socks during the 1950s. They were often given as wedding gifts and were either pat- terned with stars or textured, as for these diamond- patterned ones. They were worn by men and by women and usually shaped over the calf, as can be seen here.

I have designed the socks here with a minimal amount of shaping, but the decreases that are worked within the ribbed section cause the fabric to grip the ankle rather than form baggy folds.

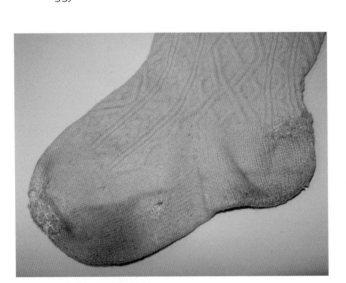

A pair of long Norwegian stockings, with shaped and intricately patterned calves and Aran-like cables on the front of the leg. Norsk Folkemuseum.

A swatch of a cabled pattern.

CONTINUOUS CABLES

Early in the 1990s, a 'new' designer emerged in Sweden: Else- beth Lavold. She came up with a way of interpreting Viking and Celtic scrollwork designs as cables. Unlike the cable motifs found in traditional Aran sweaters, these cables have multiple interlacings. Others stand alone, with loops and chains created by working increase stitches on each side of a single knit stitch.

These designs are now extremely popular in Scandinavia, as well as many other places in the world. They could be used as a design feature on pockets or in a similar way to clocks on socks.

BELOW: *Intertwining motifs on a Celtic cross in Northumberland, similar to those found on Viking ornaments.*

A close-up of the foot of the same stockings, showing the rounded heel and toe, with a few darns.

CABLED SOCKS

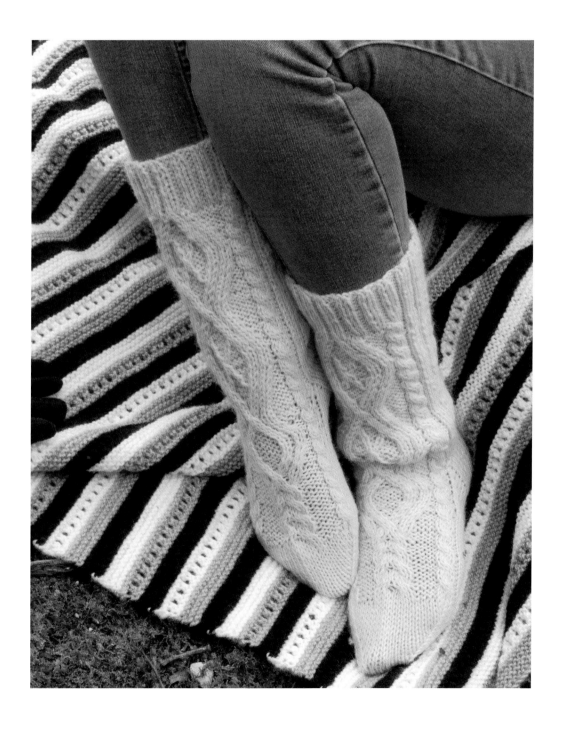

Size

To fit average adult feet

Actual measurements: leg length 12in; foot length adjustable

Materials

2 × 100g balls of DK-weight yarn

Needles

Circular 4.5mm needle (or an equivalent set of double-pointed needles)

Circular 4mm needle (or an equivalent set of double-pointed needles)

Tension

22sts and 28 rounds to 10cm/4in using 4.5mm needles over rib patt

Abbreviations

1/1 LC = slip next stitch to cable needle, place cable needle at front of work, k1 and then k1 from cable needle.

1/1 LPC = slip next stitch to cable needle, place cable needle at front of work, p1 and then k1 from cable needle.

1/1 RC = slip next stitch to cable needle, place cable needle at back of work, k1 and then k1 from cable needle.

1/1 RPC = slip next stitch to cable needle, place cable needle at back of work, k1 and then p1 from cable needle.

2/1 LPC = slip next 2 stitches to cable needle, place cable needle at front of work, p1 and then k2 from cable needle.

2/1 RPC = slip next stitch to cable needle, place cable needle at back of work, k2 and then p1 from cable needle.

For definitions and explanations of the chart's other cable symbols, see the section 'Glossary of cable and twist stitches' at the start of the book.

Leg

Using 4mm needles, cast on 76sts, join to work in the round, and work 1½in of k2, p2 rib.

Change to 4.5mm needles, and keep sts for back of leg in rib patt as follows: rib 22sts, work round 1 of cross-in-diamond chart over next 32sts, and, at the same time, inc in patt in 16th and 19th stitches of front-of-leg cable panel (to make the 34sts required to work the chart round), and rib 22sts by beg with k2. (78sts)

Work as set, following cross-in-diamond chart for rounds 2–24 for front-of-leg patt.

Next round: Rib next 22sts by working k2 sts of previous round as k2 and p2 sts of previous round as p2tog, work round 1 of cross-in-diamond chart over next 34sts, then rib next 22sts by working k2 sts of previous round as k2 and p2 sts of previous round as p2tog. (68sts)

A close-up of the raised Aran-like pattern on the instep and leg and the small cables that border this pattern.

Cross in diamond

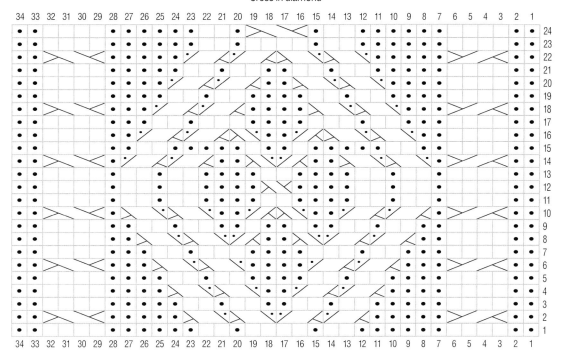

Instep cable

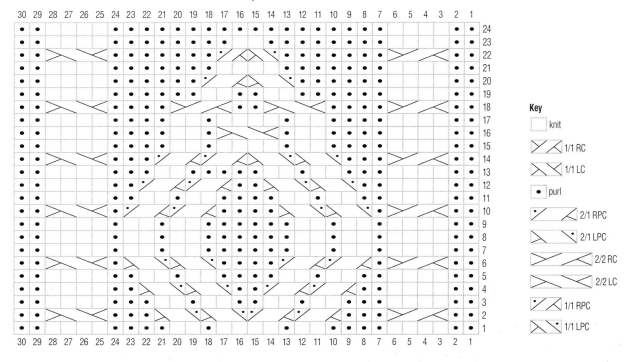

Key

knit	
1/1 RC	
1/1 LC	
• purl	
2/1 RPC	
2/1 LPC	
2/2 RC	
2/2 LC	
1/1 RPC	
1/1 LPC	

Foot

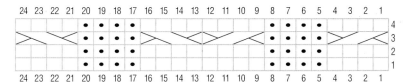

The charts for the cabled socks.

Next round: Rib next 17sts by working each knitted st of previous round as k1 and each purled st of previous round as p1, work round 2 of cross-in-diamond chart over next 34sts, then rib next 17sts by working each knitted st of previous round as k1 and each purled st of previous round as p1. Work as set, following cross-in-diamond chart for rounds 3–24 for front-of-leg patt.

Next round: Work as set, following round 1 of cross-in-diamond chart for front-of-leg patt.

Next round: Dec before starting heel as follows: rib as set to beg of front-of-leg cable panel, then p2tog, k4, p1, (p2tog) × 2, p1, k2, p1, k4, p1, k2, p1, (p2tog) ×2, p1, k4, p2tog; slip these 28sts of front of leg on to a holder for instep.

Work across all rib sts (that is, across the next 34sts, to beg of front-of-leg cable-panel sts) as follows: k1, (k1, ssk) × 10, k3. (24sts)

A view of the cross-in-diamond pattern on the front of the socks.

Next, p1 (that is, work the first stitch of the front-of-leg sts), then, at the opposite end of the group of front-of-leg sts, slip the last purl stitch to join this set of rib sts, to make 26sts.

Heel flap
Row 1: Sl1, knit to end.
Row 2: Sl1, purl to end.
Rep rows 1–2 9 times more.

Heel turn
Row 1: Sl1, k16, ssk, turn.
Row 2: Sl1, p8, p2tog, turn.
Row 3: Sl1, k8, ssk, turn.
Rep rounds 2–3 until all sts of heel flap have been worked, ending with a purl row. (10sts)
Next row: Knit across all 10sts.

Gusset
Pick up and knit 11sts down side of heel flap, then work across 26sts of instep as follows: 2/2 RC, p3, (2/1 RPC) × 2, (2/1 LPC) × 2, p3, 2/2 LC.
Pick up and knit 11sts up other side of heel flap, k5 and then pm to mark new start of round. (58sts)
Next round: K14, work round 3 of instep-cable chart over next 30sts (that is, the instep stitches and the adjacent stitch on each side), k14.
Cont in rounds as set by following instep-cable chart for instep and top of foot and working sole in st. st, and, at the same time, dec by 1 stitch before and 1 stitch after instep-cable section on alt rounds until 48sts rem.

Foot
Cont in patt by following foot chart for top of foot and working sole in st. st, until foot is 2in shorter than required length.
Next round: K9, k2tog, k2, ssk, k18, k2tog, k2, ssk, k9. (44sts)
Next round: K8, k2tog, k2, ssk, k16, k2tog, k2, ssk, k8. (40sts)
Cont to dec as set on alt rounds until 20sts rem.
Place sts corresponding to top of foot on to one needle and sts corresponding to bottom of foot on to a second needle. Graft sts together (or work three-needle cast-off with WS facing and right sides together) to close and finish sock toe.

Work second sock as for the first sock.
Weave in all yarn ends.

ROPES-AND-HOLLOWS COWL

Size

Actual measurements: depth 8in; length 27in

Materials

2 × 50g balls of Rooster Almerino Aran yarn;
50-per-cent alpaca/50-per-cent merino wool
(94m[103yd]/50g)
3 buttons, approx 2.5cm/1in in diameter

Needles

1 pair·4mm needles
1 pair 4.5mm needles

Tension

18sts and 24 rows to 10cm/4in using 4.5mm needles
over patt

Abbreviations

For definitions and explanations of the chart's cable
symbols, please see the section 'Glossary of cable and
twist stitches' at the start of the book.

A close-up of the ropes-and-hollows cable pattern.

This large interlaced cable could be used on a cowl, as in
the pattern here, or more rows could be worked to make a
scarf. Try to end the item after working a full pattern repeat
in both cases.

Using 4mm needles, cast on 54sts.
Work 10 rows of g. st.
Change to 4.5mm needles, and, keeping 3sts at each end of
every row in g. st, work the whole ropes-and-hollows chart.
If you prefer to follow written instructions, these are as
follows:

Row 1 (RS): 2/2 LC, p2, (2/2 RC, p4, 2/2 LC, p4) × 2,
2/2 RC, p2, 2/2 LC. (48sts)
Row 2 (WS): P4, k2, (p4, k4) × 4, p4, k2, p4.
Row 3: K4, p2, (k4, p3, 2/1 RPC, 2/1 LPC, p3) × 2, k4, p2,
k4.
Row 4: P4, k2, (p4, k3, p2, k2, p2, k3) × 2, p4, k2, p4.
Row 5: 2/2 LC, (p2, 2/2 RC, p2, 2/1 RPC, p2, 2/1 LPC) × 2,
p2, 2/2 RC, p2, 2/2 LC.
Row 6: P4, (k2, p4, k2, p2, k4, p2) × 2, (k2, p4) × 2.
Row 7: K4, (p2, k4, p2, k2, p4, k2) × 2, (p2, k4) × 2.
Row 8: Rep row 6.
Row 9: 2/2 LC, (p2, 2/2 RC, p2, 2/1 LPC, p2, 2/1 RPC) × 2,
p2, 2/2 RC, p2, 2/2 LC.

Row 10: Rep row 4.
Row 11: K4, p2, (k4, p3, 2/1 LPC, 2/1 RPC, p3) × 2, k4, p2,
k4.
Row 12: Rep row 2.
Row 13: 2/2 LC, p2, 2/2 RC, p4, 2/2 LC, (p4, 2/2 RC) × 3,
p2, 2/2 LC.
Row 14: Rep row 2.
Row 15: K4, p2, k2, (2/2 LPC, 2/2 RPC) × 4, k2, p2, k4.
Row 16: P4, k2, p2, k2, (p4, k4) × 3, p4, k2, p2, k2, p4.
Row 17: 2/2 LC, p2, k2, p2, 2/2 RC, p4, 2/2 LC, p4, 2/2 RC,
p4, 2/2 LC, p2, k2, p2, 2/2 LC.
Row 18: Rep row 16.
Row 19: K4, p2, k2, (2/2 RPC, 2/2 LPC) × 4, k2, p2, k4.
Row 20: Rep row 2.
Row 21: 2/2 LC, p2, (2/2 LC, p4, 2/2 RC, p4) × 2, 2/2 LC,
p2, 2/2 LC.
Row 22: Rep row 2.
Row 23: K4, p2, k2, (2/1 LPC, p3, k4, p3, 2/1 RPC) × 2, k2,
p2, k4.
Row 24: P4, k2, p2, k1, p2, k3, p4, k3, p2, k2, p2, k3, p4,
k3, p2, k1, p2, k2, p4.
Row 25: 2/2 LC, p2, k2, p1, 2/1 LPC, p2, 2/2 RC, p2,
2/1 RPC, p2, 2/1 LPC, p2, 2/2 RC, p2, 2/1 RPC, p1, k2, p2,
2/2 LC.

KEY

☐	RS: knit / WS: purl
●	RS: purl / WS: knit

⟋⟍	2/2 RC
⟍⟋	2/2 LC
⟋ (dot)	2/1 RPC
(dot) ⟍	2/1 LPC
● ⟍	2/2 RPC
⟍ ●	2/2 LPC

The ropes-and-hollows chart, which could be used for a cowl or scarf.

Row 26: P4, (k2, p2) × 2, k2, p4, k2, p2, k4, p2, k2, p4, (k2, p2) × 2, k2, p4.

Row 27: K4, (p2, k2) × 2, p2, k4, p2, k2, p4, k2, p2, k4, (p2, k2) × 2, p2, k4.

Row 28: Rep row 26.

Row 29: 2/2 LC, p2, k2, p1, 2/1 RPC, p2, 2/2 RC, p2, 2/1 LPC, p2, 2/1 RPC, p2, 2/2 RC, p2, 2/1 LPC, p1, k2, p2, 2/2 LC.

Row 30: Rep row 24.

Row 31: K4, p2, k2, (2/1 RPC, p3, k4, p3, 2/1 LPC) × 2, k2, p2, k4.

Row 32: Rep row 2.

Row 33: Rep row 21.

Row 34: Rep row 2.

Row 35: Rep row 15.

Row 36: Rep row 16.

Row 37: 2/2 LC, p2, k2, p2, 2/2 LC, p4, 2/2 RC, p4, 2/2 LC,

p4, 2/2 RC, p2, k2, p2, 2/2 LC.

Row 38: Rep row 16.

Row 39: Rep row 19.

Row 40: Rep row 2.

Cont as set until cowl measures approx 25in, preferably ending having completed row 40.

Change to 4mm needles, and work 4 rows of g. st.

Next row: Make buttonholes as follows: K7, (cast off 4sts, k11) × 2, cast off 4sts, knit to end.

Work 5 rows of g. st.

Cast off loosely.

Finishing

Weave in all yarn ends. Sew on buttons to cast-on edge to align with the buttonholes of opposite edge.

COLOURWORK

As for the pattern for the twined-knitting wristlets, twined knitting was often worked with two colours, in an attempt to copy the appearance of the early embroidered gloves of Sweden. Two-colour twined knitting was also frequently used for socks, caps and mittens. But other stranded knitting was worked in a similar fashion to that of Fair Isle knitting, with the colours being carried along the back of the work and caught in every few stitches, to prevent long floats, as described in Chapter 2.

Typical examples of Swedish colourwork are the Bjarbo and Delsbo designs, but the Halland knitting cooperative, founded by Berta Bergström, the local doctor's wife, also created their own all-over patterns. The cooperative, known as 'Binge', was started to help the women of Halland to earn money during the winter months. They collected as many patterns as they could find in the province, altered and adapted them to suit their own design principles and used these patterns mainly on stockings, mittens and double caps, that is, those that have one half tucked inside the other, as for this pattern.

DOUBLE CAP

Work the inside half in a single colour, but add patterns or stripes to the outside half, for your own version of a traditional Swedish double cap.

A double cap, with one half folded inside the other.

Size
To fit an average adult head of about 20in in circumference

Materials
2 × 50g balls of 4ply yarn in MC
1 × 50g ball of 4ply yarn in CC1
1 × 50g ball of 4ply yarn in CC2

Needles
5 double-pointed 3mm needles

Tension
30sts and 40 rows to 10cm/4in using 3mm needles over st. st

Using MC, for inside half of cap, cast on 8sts, with 2sts on each of 4 needles, and join to work in the round.
Round 1: Inc by 1 stitch in every stitch (for example, kfb around). (16sts)
Round 2 and all alt rounds: Knit.
Round 3: Inc by 1 stitch in every alt st. (24sts)
Round 5: Inc by 1 stitch in every 3rd st. (32sts)
Round 7: Inc by 1 stitch in every 4th st. (40sts)

A double cap.

Cont to inc as set until there are 144sts on the needles, and pm after each increase stitch.

Work in st. st, and slip each marker as it is reached, until piece measures 7½in from cast-on round, then introduce contrast-colour yarns (CC1 and CC2, and additional colours as preferred) and motifs as required.

When work measures 10in from beg, decrease on alt rounds by working k2tog before each marker on alt rounds until approx 8sts rem.

Finishing

Leaving a tail, cut the yarn, thread the yarn through the rem sts, draw up sts, to close the hole at top of outside half of cap, and fasten off.

Weave in all yarn ends. Tuck the plain inside half of cap into the patterned outside half. Fold back a brim, if required, and top outside half of cap with a tassel or pompom.

These double caps were usually decorated with what were termed 'traditional Halland patterns'; however, most of the patterns were common in other parts of Sweden, and some were even copied from those found in Shetland. The snow-flake-with-ferns pattern is one such pattern, worked on a slightly smaller scale. Where the knitters could not interpret the patterns correctly, they would alter them into their own designs. As this was done as early as 1910, could such patterns still be called 'traditional'?

1910 was also the date at which brightly coloured, synthetic dyes were first sold in Sweden. The knitters of Norrbotten, butting up to Finland in the northernmost area

of Sweden, adopted these dyes with abandon. They used them in their designs of mittens, stockings and sweaters, perhaps inspired by the examples of such items being sold by the Russian pedlars. The designs are often of small crosses, diamonds and rectangles, but they look very effective when worked on caps and mittens in bands of four or more bright colours. Other mittens from this area were plain cream, but with loosely stitched threads of red, white and blue, forming crosses at the cuffs. Again, like the mittens of the Sami people, they had tasselled cords at the cast-on edge and incorporated afterthought thumbs.

BOHUS KNITTING

In the 1930s, the depression hit the Bohuslän region, in particular affecting the local stone quarries, leading to high unemployment and hardship throughout the region. Women of the north of Bohuslän appealed to Emma Jacobsson, the governor´s wife; they requested that she set up a handicrafts-based industry, to help the women and their families to support themselves by working from home when they could not find other work. She agreed, and they began by making small fabric items, plus knitted socks and gloves worked in a single colour. Some items had areas of embroidery introduced, and these fetched higher prices. This led to the women deciding to concentrate on colourwork knitting, and, in 1939, the *Bohus Stickning* (Bohus Knitting) cooperative was started.

Emma, who was a talented designer herself, hired other professional designers, amongst them Vera Bjurström, Anna-Lisa Mannheimer Lunn and Kerstin Olson. These women were strict about the craftsmanship required of their knitters, and all of the outworkers attended classes before they were employed to work on the garments. Only the best yarns were used – fine, soft wool and angora – and the quality of the garments was noticed by high-class department stores around the world who were soon putting in orders for dozens of such items.

In the 1950s, every well-dressed, fashionable woman would have liked to own a Bohus twinset, cardigan or sweater. Such garments became the height of fashion, being owned by film stars such as Ingrid Bergman, which naturally made these garments even more desirable! As the designs developed, more colours were introduced, along with the distinguishing feature of Bohus knitting: the purl stitch on the right side of

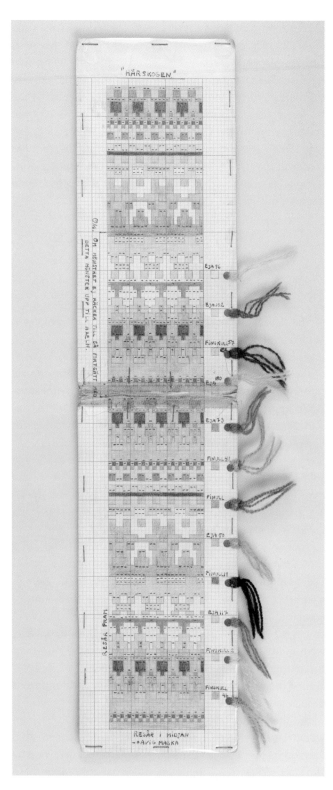

One of the particularly complete cards held by the Bohusläns Museum, showing the arrangement and shades of colours to be used for a specific garment.

the fabric. The complexity of these patterns meant that fewer people could work them, and, as the economic situation improved, it became harder to find the knitters that were skilled enough to produce them.

The Bohus Stickning cooperative existed until 1969, when, at age 84, Emma decided that changes in fashion and the increase in mass production meant that it was no longer worthwhile to produce these individually made, unique designs.

If you want to study this technique further, it is covered in a beautiful book by Wendy Keele called *Poems of Colour*.

The original Bohus-knitting garments were made by using very fine wool and angora yarns. As this is not so easy to obtain now, I have designed this cardigan pattern to be worked with DK and fine kid-mohair yarns.

The individual motifs of Bohus knitting are small, as can be seen from the chart of small Bohus patterns in Chapter 6 and the featured illustration of a combined colourwork chart and shade card. However, I have not given a chart that will exactly replicate the design of the modelled cardigan, as motifs and charts can be fairly easily combined and modified to suit your chosen yarns. It is also an interesting creative process to create a design that is unique to yourself.

BOHUS CARDIGAN

Size

Size 36, size 40 and size 44, to fit a chest circumference of 36 (40, 44)in respectively
Actual measurements: chest circumference 38 (42, 47)in; back length 22in; sleeve-seam length 17½in

Materials

400 (450, 500)g of DK-weight yarn in MC
A selection of contrast colours of kid-mohair or angora yarns or a mixture of DK-weight, kid-mohair and/or angora yarns. (I used 9 different colours of kid-mohair yarn and 2 of a contrasting DK-weight yarn).
8 buttons, approx 2cm/¾in in diameter

Needles

Circular 3.25mm needle
Circular 4mm needle
1 pair 3.25mm needles
1 pair 4mm needles

Tension

21sts and 29 rows to 10cm/4in using 4mm needles over st. st

The back of the Bohus cardigan.

Body

Worked flat as far as beg of armholes.
With MC and a circular 3.25mm needle, cast on 211 (229, 259)sts.
Work k1, p1 rib for 2½in, and, at the same time, inc by 1 stitch at end of last row. [212 (230, 260)sts]
Change to a circular 4mm needle, and work even in st. st until piece measures 15in from cast-on edge.
Pm after 52nd (58th, 65th) stitch and 160th (172nd, 195th) stitch, to mark side 'seams' of body.

Sleeves

Worked flat as far as beg of armhole.
With MC and 3.25mm needles, cast on 45 (49)sts, and work k1, p1 rib for 2in.
Change to a circular 4mm needle. Work in st. st, and, at the same time, inc by 1 stitch at each end of every 8th row until there are 71 (76, 83)sts.
Work even in st. st until piece measures 17½in from cast-on edge. Slip all sts on to a holder.

Work second sleeve as for first sleeve.

Joining body and sleeves

Transfer 2 sets of 10 (12, 14)sts [the 5 (6, 7)sts on each side of each side 'seam' marker of body] to holders for underarms.
Transfer 2 sets of 10 (12, 14)sts [the 5 (6, 7)sts from each end of each sleeve] to holders for underarms.
With RS facing, arrange and knit body and sleeve stitches with MC as follows: knit 47 (51, 57)sts of right front, 61 (64, 69)sts of right sleeve, 98 (104,116)sts of back, 61 (64, 69)sts of left sleeve and 47 (51, 57)sts of left front. [314 (334, 368)sts]
Purl 1 row.

Yoke

The following instructions are written for single-colour stocking stitch worked flat with MC, but work your chosen motifs – including purl stitches as desired – and use your chosen colours throughout the yoke, to produce your own unique design.

Decreases for the yoke are worked differently depending on the size of cardigan being worked. Because the instructions could be difficult to follow if presented together, I have separated the instructions for the different sizes.

Size 36

Work 14 rows of st. st over 314sts.
Row 15: Dec as follows to 259sts: k2, (k2tog, k3) × 8, (k2tog, k4) × 39, (k2tog, k3) × 7, k2tog, k1.
Work 12 rows of st. st over 259sts.
Row 28: Dec as follows to 204sts: p1, (p2tog, p2) × 8, (p2tog, p3) × 39, (p2tog, p2) × 7, p2tog, p1.
Work 12 rows of st. st over 204sts.
Row 41: Dec as follows to 149sts: k1, (k2tog, k1) × 8, (k2tog, k2) × 39, (k2tog, k1) × 7, k2tog, k1.
Work 12 rows of st. st over 149sts.
Row 54: Dec as follows to 94sts: p2tog × 8, (p2tog, p1) × 39, p2tog × 8.
Work 12 rows of st. st over 94sts.

Size 40

Work 14 rows of st. st over 334sts.
Row 15: Dec as follows to 273sts: (k4, k2tog, k3, k2tog × 29, (k3, k2tog) × 3.
Work 12 rows of st. st over 273sts.
Row 28: Dec as follows to 214sts: (p3, p2tog, p2, p2tog × 22, (p3, p2tog) × 15.
Work 12 rows of st. st over 214sts.
Row 41: Dec as follows to 155 stitches: (k2, k2tog, k1, k2tog × 22, (k2, k2tog) × 15.
Work 12 rows of st. st over 155sts.
Row 54: Dec as follows to 96sts: (p1, p2tog × 2) × 22, (p1, p2tog) × 15.
Work 12 rows of st. st over 96sts.

Size 44

Work 14 rows of st. st over 368sts.
Row 15: Dec as follows to 302sts: (k4, k2tog, k3, k2tog × 28, (k4, k2tog) × 10.
Work 14 rows of st. st over 302sts.
Row 30: Dec as follows to 238sts: *(p3, p2tog) × 2, p2, p2tog; rep from * 18 times, (p3, p2tog) × 10.

The colourful yoke of the Bohus cardigan.

Work 13 rows of st. st over 238sts.
Row 44: Dec as follows to 174sts: *(p2, p2tog) × 2, p1, p2tog; rep from * 18 times, (p2, p2tog) × 10.
Work 13 rows of st. st over 174sts.
Row 58: Dec as follows to 110sts: *(p1, p2tog) × 2, p2tog; rep from * 18 times, (p1, p2tog) × 10.
Work 13 rows of st. st over 110sts.

Neckband

With MC and 3.25mm needles, work 8 rows of k1, p1 rib across 94 (96, 110)sts. Cast off loosely in patt.

Front bands

With MC and a circular 3.25mm needle, pick up and knit 151 (157, 161)sts along left-front edge. Work 8 rows of k1, p1 rib. Cast off in patt.
Mark positions for 8 buttons: the first one should be ½in

above the band bottom, the last one ½in below the band top. The other positions for buttons should be evenly spaced between these two positions.

With MC and a circular 3.25mm needle, pick up and knit 151 (157, 161)sts along right-front edge. Work 3 rows of k1, p1 rib to match the left-front button band.

Next row: Cont in rib as set, and, at the same time, work preferred buttonholes at appropriate positions along the band, to correspond to the positions marked for the buttons of the left-front button band.

Work 4 rows of k1, p1 rib as set. Cast off in patt.

Finishing

Sew each sleeve seam, and, for each underarm, graft sts together (or work a three-needle cast-off with WS facing). Sew on 8 buttons.
Weave in all yarn ends.

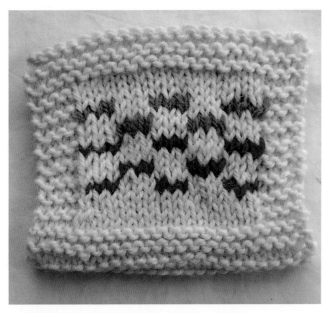

A swatch of a small-dotted-bars pattern that has been used on fishermen's jerseys. (The chart for this pattern is shown in Chapter 3.)

FISHERMEN'S SWEATERS

The Uppland area of Sweden, being a maritime province on the east coast, has a long history of fishing. As well as the beautiful, elaborate pieces of knitting that many women made for sale, they also knitted more-simple sweaters for the local fishermen. These were thick sweaters of the basic tube shape, simply decorated with textured or sometimes dotted patterns, like those that fishermen seem to have adopted all around the coasts of the northern hemisphere and similar to the pattern for the forest sweater in Chapter 3.

MODERN DESIGN

The knitting that we associate with Sweden today is most likely to be that which is known as 'homeware'; cushions, throws and other domestic furnishings. The Stockholm Exhibition of 1930 displayed many such classic designs, with their clean and simple lines. Many of the knitted pieces are predominantly white or light grey, to give the effect of providing light during the long, dark winters. At the same time, they give off a feeling of cosiness and warmth, and throws made of natural wool or mohair are particularly popular.

These days, some of the pieces are made with extra-bulky wool on huge needles, or they feature large, chunky cables. The ideal is to combine functionality with comfort and sustainability; pieces should be made well with quality materials, made to last a long time and made to give pleasure to the owner. The Danish word '*hygge*' has come to be associated with this style. Geometric patterns appear on all manner of items, which is especially useful for knitters, as instructions for such patterns are easy to follow and adapt. The throw and cushion patterns here have one of the simplest patterns of all: a series of stripes in black, grey and white.

CUSHION COVER AND THROW

Size

Throw actual measurements: 40in × 60in (approx), requiring 400g of yarn

Cushion-cover actual measurements: 16in square, requiring 150g of yarn

Materials

3 × 100g balls of DK-weight yarn in grey
2 × 100g balls of DK-weight yarn in white
2 × 100g balls of DK-weight yarn in black
1 cushion pad, 16in square
1 zip, approx 12in long

Needles

1 pair 4mm needles

Tension

20sts and 36 rows to 10cm/4in using 4mm needles over st. st; however, note that matching this tension is not vital for these items

Clean lines and a neutral palette for a typical Swedish design.

For a classic Swedish style, choose calm, muted colours. For example, this throw and cushion cover could be made in pastel shades or in the natural colours of sheep's wool.

Throw

Using grey and 4mm needles, cast on 161sts.
Knit 8 rows with grey.
Begin stripe pattern:
Using white:
Rows 1–3: Knit.
Row 4: K1, (yo, p2tog) to end.
Rows 5–6: Knit.

Using black: Knit 6 rows.
Using grey: Work as for rows 1–6.
Using white: Knit 6 rows.
Using black: Work as for rows 1–6.
Using grey: Knit 6 rows.
Rep these 36 rows of stripe pattern until work measures approx 60in from cast-on edge.
Knit 8 rows with the appropriate colour to cont the established grey–white–black sequence.
Cast off.

Cushion cover

Using grey and 4mm needles, cast on 71sts.
Work as for throw until piece measures 16in from cast-on edge.
Using grey, work 16in of g. st.

Finishing

Fold cushion cover in half, at the boundary between patterned and grey-only halves of the fabric. Sew both side seams, then sew top seam, leaving a gap for the zip.
Sew in zip.
Weave in all yarn ends, and insert cushion pad.

The Viking-scrollwork cowl, with its button fastenings.

The Swedish word 'lagom', loosely translated as 'everything in moderation', could be the ethos that informs your own design. Lagom is similar in meaning to the Danish word *hygge*, but, as well as being associated with the importance of physical and intangible things being cosy and comfortable, *lagom* suggests that contentment comes from living a more frugal life. Everything in the home should serve a function without being superfluous; only take as much as you need, and leave something for others. Use sustainable materials where possible, and recycle your hand-knitted items as they become worn. Whereas *hygge* can refer to a few moments, lagom is a way of life in general.

CHAPTER 5

DENMARK AND THE FAROE ISLANDS

Denmark was probably the first of the Scandinavian countries to produce garments by using the technique of knitting with two needles. There was a cottage industry from at least the seventeenth century, mainly for the production of undergarments, stockings, mittens and leggings. These were taken to the markets in Copenhagen to be sold to buyers from other areas of Scandinavia and, possibly, elsewhere in mainland Europe.

A collection of knitting sheaths of various shapes and sizes, similar in shape to that of the 'knitting peg' held in a Danish museum.

The National Museum of Denmark has a silver knitting tool dated to the late sixteenth century. It is similar in shape to the wooden knitting sheaths used by the knitters of Britain who were known as 'the terrible knitters of Dent', who knitted to supplement their income and were famed for their speed, indicating that perhaps there may have been similar employment of outworkers in Denmark as early as that time.

NIGHTSHIRTS (*NATTROJER*)

The most distinctive item of Danish knitwear is that of the T-shaped garment known as a *nattroje* or nightshirt. They were often made from silk and as such were mainly worn by royalty. Because they are made from silk, they are very fragile, and any that are held by museums are not put out on display for fear of them disintegrating further. They were similar in shape to the British and Dutch fisherman's ganseys and often featured patterns of diamonds, similar to the design of Charles II's brocade vest or the pattern that is featured on this little boy's sweater.

Although these garments were termed 'nightshirts', they were often kept on and worn as underwear through the day. Later, as fashions changed through the nineteenth century,

A gansey-inspired sweater, with a simple design of half-diamond chevron shapes.

A swatch of the Danish-stars pattern, a motif related to the Norwegian star.

men wore similar items as hip-length jackets, and women wore them as layers, as we would nowadays wear a sweater, often under a cloth bodice.

They were of a cropped style, knitted in the round, with the hem, often of a basket-weave or chequerboard-type pattern, knitted separately as two pieces and then joined to be worked with the rest of the body in the round. Most of the

early knitting was made in this way, just like the fishermen's ganseys: in the round as far as the armholes, then divided for the back and front to be worked flat to the shoulders.

The jumpers were knitted in white and then dyed when completed, usually in red, blue or green. The oldest piece of knitting found in Denmark is a fragment of one such garment. It is dyed blue, most likely with indigo, and has a pattern of stars and diagonal lines worked with purl stitches.

Some areas of Denmark produced garments with decorative knitted sleeves attached to cloth bodices, and many had embroidered silk facings at the neckline. One of

A typical *nattroje*

The hem was invariably knitted as two flat pieces, often in a pattern of four knit and four purl stitches worked around for four rows and then alternated to form a textured check or basket-weave design. The pieces were then joined together and knitted in the round. The lower part was often left plain, apart from one or two purl stitches to mark each side seam. You can see that this idea is continued today in the fisherman's gansey. Next, there would be a patterned section of stars or a variation of them, like the featured pattern from the fragment of knitting found in Denmark. Above the armholes, the work would be knitted back and forth. At the front would be a square neckline, with the top and side edges being worked with a non-

curling pattern of rib or moss stitch. The back would have a straight neck edge of the same stitch as used for the front. The shoulders were joined by the knitting, grafting or sewing together of the front- and back-shoulder stitches. The sleeve cuffs or the fabric of the whole sleeves would have a star pattern, sometimes different to that of the bodice, and they would be knitted in the round from the cuff upwards, to be sewn into the armholes.

They were knitted in fine wool yarn on small needles, often at a tension of 8 stitches to the inch! Some *nattrojer* had a mini version of the star pattern along the line of the side seams, and a few of these motifs can be seen in Chapter 6.

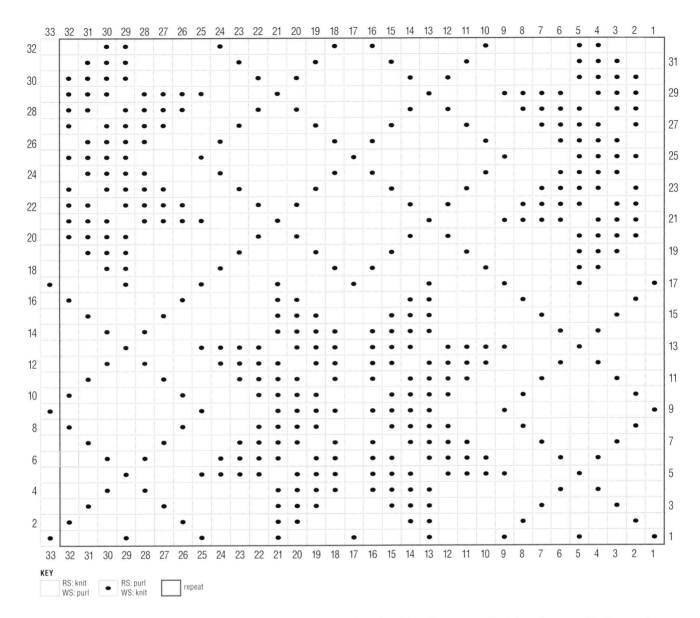

The Danish-stars chart, for the stars-and-diamonds pattern found on the oldest fragment of knitting discovered in Denmark.

the unique aspects of Danish knitting is that, in some parts, the garments were dyed different colours, depending on what they were intended for; for example, green was for everyday use and red for feast days. Blue was an expensive dye and so was mainly used for items for special occasions. Women also wore knitted underskirts, usually fairly plain, but that occasionally had similar motifs to those used for *nattrøjer* knitted into them. They were frequently dyed red.

The pattern for a nightshirt was most likely drawn out as a series of dots, as demonstrated in the featured example, with each dot representing a purl stitch, or marked on squared paper as for a cross-stitch pattern. I have made the chart for the Danish-stars pattern by using modern charting software called Stitchmastery. I have also written out the instructions here for anyone who is not fond of charts!

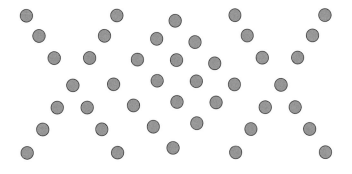

An example of how the early knitters may have drawn 'charts' for themselves and possibly how they may have appeared in the printed books of the nineteenth century.

Danish-stars written instructions

Row 1 (RS): *(P1, k3) × 8; work from * to last st, p1. (33sts)

Row 2 (WS): P1, *k1, p5, k1, p4, k2, p5, k2, p4, k1, p5, k1, p1; work from * to end of row.

Row 3: *K2, p1, k3, p1, k5, p3, k3, p3, k5, p1, k3, p1, k1; work from * to last st, k1.

Row 4: P1, *p2, k1, p1, k1, p6, k4, p1, k4, p6, k1, p1, k1, p3; work from * to end of row.

Row 5: *K4, p1, k3, p4, (k1, p3) × 2, k1, p4, k3, p1, k3; work from * to last st, k1.

Row 6: P1, *p2, k1, p1, k1, p3, k4, (p1, k2) × 2, p1, k4, p3, k1, p1, k1, p3; work from * to end of row.

Row 7: *K2, (p1, k3) × 2, p4, (k1, p1) × 2, k1, p4, (k3, p1) × 2, k1; work from * to last st, k1.

Row 8: P1, *k1, p5, k1, (p3, k4) × 2, p3, k1, p5, k1, p1; work from * to end of row.

Row 9: *P1, k7, p1, k3, p4, k1, p4, k3, p1, k7, p1; work from * to last st, p1.

Row 10: Rep row 8.

Row 11: Rep row 7.

Row 12: Rep row 6.

Row 13: Rep row 5.

Row 14: Rep row 4.

Row 15: Rep row 3.

Row 16: Rep row 2.

Row 17: Rep row 1.

Row 18: P1, *p2, k2, p4, k1, p5, k1, p1, k1, p5, k1, p4, k2, p3; work from * to end of row.

Row 19: *K2, p3, k5, (p1, k3) × 3, p1, k5, p3, k1; work from * to last st, k1.

Row 20: P1, *k4, p6, k1, p1, k1, p5, k1, p1, k1, p6, k4, p1; work from * to end of row.

Row 21: *K1, p3, k1, p4, k3, p1, k7, p1, k3, p4, k1, p3; work from * to last st, k1.

Row 22: P1, *k2, p1, k4, p3, k1, p1, k1, p5, k1, p1, k1, p3, k4, p1, k2, p1; work from * to end of row.

Row 23: *K1, p1, k1, p4, (k3, p1) × 4, k3, p4, k1, p1; work from * to last st, k1.

Row 24: P1, *p1, k4, p3, k1, p5, k1, p1, k1, p5, k1, p3, k4, p2; work from * to end of row.

Row 25: *K1, p4, k3, (p1, k7) × 2, p1, k3, p4; work from * to last st, k1.

Row 26: Rep row 24.

Row 27: Rep row 23.

Row 28: Rep row 22.

Row 29: Rep row 21.

Row 30: Rep row 20.

Row 31: Rep row 19.

Row 32: Rep row 18.

SOCKS

The textured patterns used for the nightshirts and other garments were often also used on knitted socks. Perhaps a small column of a stars pattern would be repeated along the outside of the leg or one star or snowflake would be intertwined with tendrils, leading down into the gusset shaping. The knitting of socks was seen as the sign of a good housewife, and the subject of wives occupied with their knitting was depicted in paintings from the early nineteenth century. The socks were usually being knitted in the round on four needles and by using white wool: another symbol of purity and devotion! The home and a happy, industrious family life were the ideal for Denmark at that time, and the knitting of socks appeared to exemplify it.

GANSEYS

As for many seafaring nations, Denmark's sailors and fishermen often wore the plain, tube-like sweater known as a gansey; the name possibly derived from the old Norse word

Another variation of a dotted pattern, worked in bands of two colours.

A Shetland shawl.

'*geansai*'. Similar patterns of knit and purl stitches to those found on the nightshirts are often seen on the yokes of the ganseys of Denmark, but for the most part they are more simple patterns of various forms of moss stitch.

Interestingly, many of these knit-and-purl, seeded patterns were also worked with two colours in place of the knit and purl stitches; red or blue on white backgrounds, sometimes alternating to red and blue in bands. These colourwork patterns would be worked throughout in stocking stitch.

SHAWLS

Another familiar garment worn by Danish women was the shawl (*kællingesjal*). The typical Danish shawl is similar in appearance to the hap shawl worn in the Shetland Islands, but in this instance the fabric is worked as a half triangle.

It was large enough to fold around the body and have the ends tied at the back. This helped it to stay in place and not have ends dangling in the way while working. The main part would be knit in garter stitch or a not-very-elaborate pattern in a combination of knits and purls; this would then be edged with a lace border that was flexible enough to stretch along the outer edges and around the lowest point of the triangle of the shawl and to allow the shawl to be tied at the front or back to keep the ends from dangling in the way. The pattern here is inspired by one dated to 1897 and held in a Danish museum. They were frequently worn by the fishwives who sold their wares in the market in Gammel Strand in Copehagen. These

A view showing the typical triangular shape of the Danish shawl.

women's market stalls were open to the North Sea, and while at the market these fishwives often wore newspapers wrapped around their chests, as well as lots of clothes on top! In Copenhagen, there is a statue of a fishwife who is depicted wearing one of these shawls.

SONNTAG SHAWL

Size

Actual measurements: wingspan 72in; length 35in

Materials

250g of Shetland 4ply yarn

Needles

1 pair 3.5mm needles

Tension

20sts and 32 rows to 10cm/4in using 4mm needles over g. st

Garter tab

Begin shawl with a garter tab, worked as follows: with 3.5mm needles, cast on 3sts, and knit 9 rows.

At the end of the last row, without turning the work, rotate the knitting clockwise through 90 degrees, and pick up and knit 7sts along the long, now-horizontal side of the fabric, again rotate the knitting clockwise through 90 degrees, and pick up and knit 3sts from the cast-on edge (13sts).

Shawl body

Row 1: K13.
Row 2: (K3, yo) × 2, k1, (yo, k3) × 2.
Row 3: K17, and mark centre stitch.
Row 4: K3, yo, knit to marker, yo, knit marked st, yo, knit to last 3sts, yo, k3.

Cont in g. st in this way, increasing by 4sts on every alt row by working yo sts as set, until work measures 10in from garter tab down the shawl centre, ending with WS facing, having completed a RS row.

**Work 10 rows of st. st, beg with a purl row, keeping 3sts at each end in g. st and cont to inc as set.

Work 10 rows of rev. st. st, keeping 3sts at each end in g. st and cont to inc as set.

Rep from ** once more.

Work 10 rows of st. st, keeping 3sts at each end in g. st and cont to inc as set.

Cont in g. st and cont to inc as set, until work measures 25in (or length required) from garter tab down the shawl centre, ending with RS facing, having completed a RS row.

Leave all stitches on the needle: do not break off yarn.

Lace edging

Add lace edging by working from edging chart or written instructions; on all WS rows, the last stitch of the edging is purled together with the stitch of the shawl body that is closest to the point of the left-hand needle (that is, a p2tog is worked with one edging stitch and one shawl-body stitch). Note that the number of shawl-body stitches needs to be a multiple of 6 minus 1 stitch, in order for complete repeats of the 12-row lace-edging pattern to be worked along the shawl edge. Any extra stitches can be dealt with by working a p3tog decrease instead of a p2tog decrease at the end of one or more WS rows.

With RS facing, cast on 25sts at end of last row.
Row 1 (WS; set-up row): K24, p2tog. (25sts)
Row 2 (RS): Sl1, k2, (yo, ssk) × 10, yo, k2. (26sts)
Row 3: K25, p2tog.
Row 4: Sl1, k5, (yo, ssk) × 9, yo, k2. (27sts)
Row 5: K26, p2tog.
Row 6: Sl1, k8, (yo, ssk) × 8, yo, k2. (28sts)

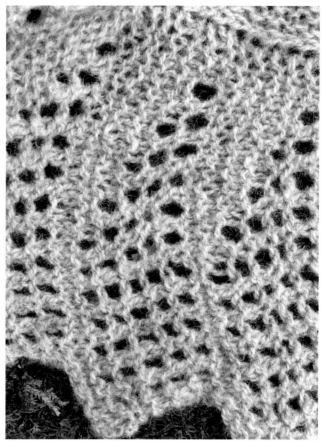

A close-up of the sonntag-shawl edging.

Lace edging

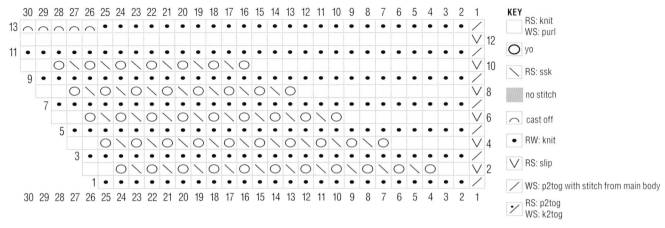

The edging charts for the Danish sonntag shawl.

A close-up of the different bands of stocking stitch, reverse stocking stitch and garter stitch at the centre of the shawl.

Row 7: K27, p2tog.
Row 8: Sl1, k11, (yo, ssk) × 7, yo, k2. (29sts)
Row 9: K28, p2tog.
Row 10: Sl1, k14, (yo, ssk) × 6, yo, k2. (30sts)
Row 11: K29, p2tog.
Row 12: Sl1, k29.
Row 13: Cast off 5sts, k24, p2tog. (25sts)
Rep rows 2–13 until all shawl-body sts are worked off.
Weave in all yarn ends, and block your shawl as described in Chapter 2. Shawls, especially, benefit from a firm wet blocking.

For a shallower and slightly curved lace edging, follow the accompanying alternative-lace-edging chart or use the following written instructions:
Note that the number of shawl-body stitches needs to be a multiple of 7 minus 1, in order for complete repeats of the 14-row lace-edging pattern to be worked along the shawl edge. Any extra stitches can be dealt with by working a p3tog decrease instead of a p2tog decrease at the end of one or more WS rows.

With RS facing, cast on 15sts at end of last row.
Set-up row (WS): Knit 1 row, purling the last stitch together with one from the shawl body, then work as follows:
Row 1 (RS): K2, yo, p2tog, k7, yo, k2tog, k2.
Row 2: P11, yo, p2tog, k1, p2tog.
Row 3: K2, yo, p2tog, k3, k2tog, k2, (yo, k2tog) × 2.
Row 4: P10, yo, p2tog, k1, p2tog.
Row 5: K2, yo, p2tog, k2, k2tog, k2, yo, k2tog, k2.

Alternative lace edging

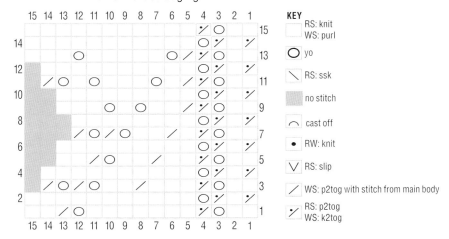

KEY

(blank)	RS: knit / WS: purl
O	yo
\	RS: ssk
(shaded)	no stitch
⌒	cast off
•	RW: knit
V	RS: slip
/	WS: p2tog with stitch from main body
✓	RS: p2tog / WS: k2tog

Row 6: P9, yo, p2tog, k1, p2tog.

Row 7: K2, yo, p2tog, k1, k2tog, k2, (yo, k2tog) × 2.

Row 8: P8, yo, p2tog, k1, p2tog.

Row 9: K2, yo, p2tog, k2tog k2, yo, k1, yo, k3.

Row 10: P9, yo, p2tog, k1, p2tog.

Row 11: K2, yo, p2tog, k2tog, k1, yo, k3, yo, k1, yo, k2tog.

Row 12: P10, yo, p2tog, k1, p2tog.

Row 13: K2, yo, p2tog, k2tog, yo, k5, yo, k3.

Row 14: P11, yo, p2tog, k1, p2tog.

Rep rows 1–14 until all shawl-body sts are worked off.

Weave in all yarn ends, and block your shawl as described in Chapter 2.

GLOVES AND MITTENS

As for the inhabitants of other Scandinavian countries, the Danes also wore – and still wear – gloves and mittens. There is a pair of gloves in the National Museum of Denmark with a motif similar to one of the lozenge shapes seen in Fair Isle knitting but worked in solid blocks of green, red, blue and white. This motif may well have been imported, but similar designs are also seen on gloves and mittens knitted in Denmark. They are frequently trimmed with fringes of colour at the cuffs and sometimes have the tips of the fingers knitted in one of the colours used for the colourwork sections of the mittens.

Two Scandinavian ladies with their warm, woolly knitwear.

HOT-WATER-BOTTLE COVER

Size

Actual measurements: circumference 16in; length 13in

Materials

2 × 50g ball of DK-weight yarn in MC

2 × 50g ball of DK-weight yarn in CC1

1 × 50g ball of DK-weight yarn each in CC2 and CC3

Needles

Circular 4.5mm needle

Circular 4mm needle

Tension

23sts and 25 rows to 10cm/4in using 4.5mm needles over colourwork patt

The large star or snowflake that is seen throughout the rest of Scandinavia was often also employed in Denmark, sometimes alone in bands across the body of a sweater or sometimes outlined with smaller motifs, as in this pattern for a hot-water-bottle cover.

Using MC and a circular 4.5mm needle, cast on 84sts, and join to work in the round.
Work 6 rows in MC, then work from the dots-and-crosses and diamonds charts, placing the corresponding motifs as demonstrated in the accompanying illustrations.
When the dots-and-crosses and diamonds charts are complete, increase evenly to 88 stitches.

Work large-snowflake chart. When it is completed, work 1 row of MC, and, at the same time, dec to 84sts.

Dots and crosses

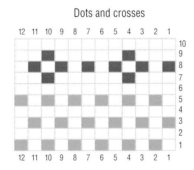

Diamonds

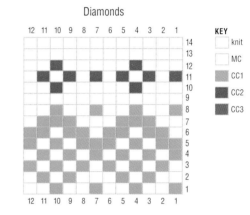

KEY

☐	knit
☐	MC
▨	CC1
■	CC2
▩	CC3

The charts for the hot-water-bottle cover.

Large snowflake

Work rows 9–14 of diamonds charts, then work whole diamonds chart.

Cont in st. st with MC until work measures approx 11in from cast-on edge.

Change to using a circular 4mm needle, and work 5 rounds of k1, p1 rib in MC.

Eyelets

*K1, yo, k2tog, p1; rep from * to end.

Work 8 rounds more of k1, p1 rib.

Cast off loosely in patt.

Finishing

Make a twisted cord, and thread cord through the eyelets. Weave in all yarn ends.

An example of domino knitting, showing how the squares look when joined together.

DOMINO KNITTING

In 2002, Vivian Høxbro published a book, *Knit To Be Square*, with patterns worked with the technique of what she calls 'domino knitting'. This is a technique for knitting squares, or rectangles, that are joined together as you go, by picking up stitches along one of the edges of a previously made square (or rectangle) and casting on a few more stitches to begin the next square (or rectangle). It is a technique of joining blocks of knitting without the need for sewing them together; each new block is constructed from stitches that are picked up from the previous one, sometimes with the addition of extra stitches to form a larger shape.

This is not a new technique; it has been practised in Denmark for the making of blankets for many years, and it is also known there as 'patchwork knitting'. It was spotted by Vivian at a craft fair in Germany, and she subsequently wrote a book explaining the technique and giving a number of patterns. It is usually worked entirely in garter stitch, but, for added interest, some rows can be worked in stocking stitch. Be wary, though, of including too many stocking-stitch rows, as, because the number of rows and stitches for a given length measurement is not equal for stocking stitch, as it is for garter stitch, the decreases won't end up forming a square.

A close-up of the hot-water-bottle cover, showing the motifs more clearly.

First square

Cast on an odd number of stitches for the first square (for example, the one at bottom left in the illustration). Knit one row, and place a stitch marker before the centre group of three stitches, and slip the marker every time it is reached on subsequent rows. On the next and every alternate row, knit together these three stitches following the marker, until all of the stitches are worked off (resulting in one stitch being present on the right-hand needle).

Subsequent squares

For square 2, pick up and knit half the number of stitches that you cast on for square 1 along the top of square 1. Then, cast on this number of stitches plus one. Work this square, square 2, as for square 1. Square 3 is worked by casting on half the number of stitches that you cast on for square 1 plus one and then picking up the rest of the stitches along the right-hand side of square 1. It will be obvious how to work square 4 and any subsequent squares.

MAGIC BALL

Another inspirational Danish designer is Christel Seyfarth. She designs brightly coloured shawls as well as coats and jackets featuring a technique called 'magic ball'. This technique results in a similar effect to that of working with the colour-changing balls of yarn that are available now, but you can make one yourself from your oddments of yarn left over from previously used balls, skeins, cakes and cones. It is a bit time-consuming but is a useful way of using up stash. Try to use yarns that are all of the same yarn weight, but they don't have to be all of the same fibre; in fact, working this technique looks most effective if some are mohair and some smooth wool yarns are used.

Making a magic ball

Break off multiple long lengths – 4 to 5 yards or more – of yarn (but don't make them all of the same length!). Thread a needle with one of the yarns. Insert the threaded needle between the plies and into the yarn that it is threaded with

a couple of inches along its length, to make a loop. With a second needle threaded with the second length of yarn, pass this threaded needle through the loop created in the first length of yarn before splitting the plies of the second yarn and running this needle through it a couple of inches along its length (as previously). You have just chain linked the first and second yarns together. Continue doing this, to chain link together more lengths of yarn, until you have enough linked yarn to form into a magic ball to start knitting with.

An attractive way to work with these magic-ball yarns is to make one yarn with dark colours and another with light ones. One will be for the main (background) colour and the other will be for working the motifs of a pattern. Make these magic-ball yarns with a strong colour contrast between them for the most effective results.

There are also yarns made in Denmark by Kauni that contain long sections of graded colours that can be knitted into beautifully colourful garments without the need for joining yarn or stranding colours. They would be ideal for making domino blankets or jumpers with bands of geometrical motifs.

TEXTURED KNITTING

Other traditional knitted items to be found in Denmark were the long jackets with all-over patterns of flowers, birds or stars worked in purl stitches on a knitted background. These sometimes had additional pieces of unspun wool (thrums) caught in on the inside of the item, to give extra thickness and warmth. As noted elsewhere, many of these designs evolved from Dutch knitting patterns.

In 1919, in Herning, Denmark, Søren Nielsen Skyt (1899–1972) began selling knitted sweaters, intended as warm, hard-wearing sweaters for fishermen. They were of the same basic shape as of a gansey but had patterns of what he called 'bobbles', which had extra insulating properties. These sweaters were worked on machines by using a tuck-stitch technique and are still produced today by the company S. N. S. Herning.

Nevertheless, for warm, hand-knitted garments, the Danes often used fabric incorporating travelling stitches, which are also found in the knitwear of Austria and Bavaria and were possibly copied from the knitwear items of these countries that were imported into Denmark. The stitches are usually crossed over only two stitches, as in the pattern for this textured sweater, but sometimes three.

ESBJERG DROP-SHOULDERED SWEATER WITH TRAVELLING STITCHES

Size

To fit a chest circumference of 34 (38, 40)in

Materials

15 (16, 18) × 50g balls of Rooster Almerino Aran yarn; 50-per-cent alpaca/50-per-cent merino wool (94m[103yd]/50g)

Needles

1 pair 3.75mm needles
1 pair 4.5mm needles

Tension

24sts and 28 rows to 10cm/4in using 4.5mm needles over travelling-stitch-diamonds patt

Abbreviations

tw2L = twist 2sts left; knit into the back of the second stitch on the left-hand needle, but do not remove this stitch from the left-hand needle; now, knit into the front of the first stitch on the left-hand needle; and, finally, slip both worked stitches off of the left-hand needle. (Note that this is nearly equivalent to working a 1/1 LC.)
tw2R = twist 2sts right; knit 2 stitches together (k2tog), but do not remove these stitches from the left-hand needle; now, knit into the front of the first stitch on the left-hand needle, and slip both worked stitches off of the left-hand needle. (Note that this is nearly equivalent to working a 1/1 RC.)

For definitions and explanations of the chart's cable symbols, see the section 'Glossary of cable and twist stitches' at the start of the book.

KEY

RS: knit / WS: purl   ● RS: purl / WS: knit   ⟋⟍ 2twR   ⟍⟋ 2twL   ☐ repeat

The chart for the textured Esbjerg sweater.

Travelling-stitch-diamonds written instructions

Row 1 (WS): P2 (5, 2), k2, (k2, p2, k4, p2, k2) × 8 (8, 9), k2, p2 (5, 2). [104 (110, 116) sts]
Row 2 (RS): K0 (3, 0), 1/1 RC, k2, (k2, 1/1 LC, k4, 1/1 RC, k2) × 8 (8, 9), k2, 1/1 LC, k0 (3, 0).
Row 3: Rep row 1.
Row 4: Knit.
Row 5: Rep row 1.
Row 6: Rep row 2.
Row 7: Rep row 1.
Row 8: K1 (4, 1), 1/1 LC, k1, (k1, 1/1 RC, k6, 1/1 LC, k1) × 8 (8, 9), k1, 1/1 RC, k1 (4, 1).
Row 9: P3 (6, 3), k1, (k1, p3, k4, p3, k1) × 8 (8, 9), k1, p3 (6, 3).
Row 10: K2 (5, 2), 1/1 LC, (1/1 RC, k8, 1/1 LC) × 8 (8, 9), 1/1 RC, k2 (5, 2).
Row 11: P4 (7, 4), (p4, k4, p4) × 8 (8, 9), p4 (7, 4).
Row 12: K3 (6, 3), (1/1 RC, k10) × 8 (8, 9), 1/1 RC, k3 (6, 3).
Row 13: Rep row 11.
Row 14: K2 (5, 2), 1/1 RC, (1/1 LC, k8, 1/1 RC) × 8 (8, 9), 1/1 LC, k2 (5, 2).
Row 15: Rep row 9.
Row 16: K1 (4, 1), 1/1 RC, k1, (k1, 1/1 LC, k6, 1/1 RC, k1) × 8 (8, 9), k1, 1/1 LC, k1 (4, 1).
Row 17: Rep row 1.

A close-up of the textured pattern and crossing of the travelling stitches of the Esbjerg sweater.

Row 18: K0 (3, 0), 1/1 LC, k2, (k2, 1/1 RC, k4, 1/1 LC, k2) × 8 (8, 9), k2, 1/1 RC, k0 (3, 0).

Row 19: Rep row 1.

Row 20: Knit.

Row 21: Rep row 1.

Row 22: Rep row 18.

Row 23: Rep row 1.

Row 24: K4 (7, 4), (k3, 1/1 LC, k2, 1/1 RC, k3) × 8 (8, 9), k4 (7, 4).

Row 25: P2 (5, 2), k2, ((k2, p3) × 2, k2) × 8 (8, 9), k2, p2 (5, 2).

Row 26: K4 (7, 4), (k4, 1/1 LC, 1/1 RC, k4) × 8 (8, 9), k4 (7, 4).

Row 27: P2 (5, 2), k2, (k2, p8, k2) × 8 (8, 9), k2, p2 (5, 2).

Row 28: K4 (7, 4), (k5, 1/1 LC, k5) × 8 (8, 9) times, k4 (7, 4).

Row 29: Rep row 27.

Row 30: K4 (7, 4), (k4, 1/1 RC, 1/1 LC, k4) × 8 (8, 9), k4 (7, 4).

Row 31: Rep row 25.

Row 32: K4 (7, 4), (k3, 1/1 RC, k2, 1/1 LC, k3) × 8 (8, 9), k4 (7, 4).

Back

Using 3.75mm needles, cast on 100 (106, 112)sts, and work in rib patt as follows:

Row 1 (RS): P1, (tw2R, p1) to end.

Row 2 (WS): K1, (tw2Lp, k1) to end.

Rep rows 1–2 until work measures 3in from cast-on edge, ending with RS facing, having completed a WS row.

Next row: Knit across row, and, at the same time, inc evenly to 104 (110, 116)sts.

Using 4.5mm needles, work travelling-stitch-diamonds patt by following the accompanying chart or written instructions until piece measures 24 (25, 26)in from cast-on edge, ending with RS facing, having completed a WS row. Note that, if you are working the second size (to fit a chest circumference of 38in) from the chart, three additional stocking-stitch stitches must be worked at the start and at the end of every row. On a WS row, p3, work across the row as directed by the chart, then p3; on a RS row, k3, work across the row as directed by the chart, then k3. (The written instructions for the travelling-stitch-diamonds patt account for these additional stocking-stitch stitches.)

Cast off 18 (19, 20)sts at beg of next 4 rows.

Slip rem 36 (38, 40)sts on to a holder for back neck.

A neat side seam of the Esbjerg sweater.

Front

Work as for back until piece measures 20 (21, 22)in from cast-on edge, ending with RS facing, having completed a WS row.

Neck shaping

For left front, work across first 49 (51, 53)sts in travelling-stitch-diamonds patt, and turn. Cont to follow patt, and, at the same time, dec by 1 stitch at neck edge of next 10 rows and then at same edge of alt rows until 36 (38, 40)sts rem. Work even for 3 rows in patt, ending with RS facing, having completed a WS row.

Shoulder shaping

Cast off 18 (19, 20)sts at beg of next and following alt row. Return to rem sts of front, and, with RS facing, place 10 (11, 12)sts closest to neck edge on to a holder for front neck. Rejoin yarn to neck edge of right front, work across 49 (51, 53)sts in travelling-stitch-diamonds patt, and turn. Cont to follow patt, and, at the same time, dec by 1 stitch at neck edge of next 10 rows and then at same edge of alt rows until 36 (38, 40)sts rem.
Work even for 3 rows, ending with WS facing, having completed a RS row.
Cast off 18 (19, 20)sts at beg of next and following alt row.

Shoulder seaming
Sew both shoulder seams, to join left front and right front to back.

Sleeves

Using 3.75mm needles, cast on 58sts, and work in rib patt as for back until piece measures 3in from cast-on edge, ending with RS facing, having completed a WS row.
Change to 4.5mm needles, and work in travelling-stitch-diamonds patt as for back, starting at row 2, as follows: k5, (tw2R, k4, tw2L, k4) × 4, knit to end.
This row sets the correct position of patt.
Cont in patt as set, and, at the same time, inc at each end of every 6th row, taking increase sts into g. st, until there are 80 (86, 90)sts.
Work even in patt until piece measures 17in from cast-on edge.
Cast off.

A cosy, everyday sweater, ideal for cool conditions.

Work second sleeve as for first sleeve.

Neckband

Using a circular 3.75mm needle and with RS facing, pick up and knit 1 stitch from left shoulder seam and 21sts along left-front neck edge, knit 10 (11, 12)sts from front-neck holder, pick up and knit 21sts along right-front neck edge and 1 stitch from right shoulder seam, and knit 36 (38, 40) sts from back-neck holder. [90 (93, 96)sts]
Row 1: P1, k2 around.
Row 2: P1, tw2R around.
Rep row 2 for 6 rounds more.
Cast off in patt.

Finishing

Sew cast-off edges of sleeves into separate armholes. Sew both side seams and sleeve seams, and weave in all yarn ends.

HYGGE

In the last chapter, there were references to *hygge* in connection with Denmark. This term doesn't have a direct translation into English but seems to project a feeling or mood: a feeling of well-being and contentment where the air is warm and comfortable, with no harsh jarring of the senses. Denmark is frequently referred to as a happy country, and this is because *hygge* seems to define the character of the Danish people and their attitude to life. Because of the long days of cold weather in Denmark, there is a focus on indoors and the home. The attraction of *hygge* may be that it is a way of enjoying simple and inexpensive pleasures such as candlelight, aesthetically pleasing furniture and decoration, and socializing with friends but also the cosiness and warmth of hand knitting, especially thick knitted sweaters and socks, cushions, blankets and throws. These items of homeware are often made from thick yarn, or even roving (unspun wool), worked on very large needles; preferably, this yarn would be from a natural source, as *hygge* also means connecting to nature. But, above all, the knitted items should be soft and comforting and ideally made from a quality wool such as merino or a cashmere blend. If an item isn't soft and warm then it won't be *hygge*.

FAROE ISLANDS (FAROES)

The name 'Faroes' is said to mean 'Sheep Island', although it is actually a group of eighteen small islands. This designation tells you that wool and knitting played an important part in the economy of the islands. Being out in the Atlantic means it is wet, windy and cold; these conditions naturally require the people who live and work there to have warm clothing.

The native sheep were similar to those of Shetland: small and hardy and with fleeces in various shades of browns, greys and whites. Like the wool of Shetland sheep, their wool can be plucked; often, the sheep rub it off themselves, and this would have been gathered, carded – but left unwashed – and then spun. Strong, hairy wool and softer, finer wool are both found on the same sheep, and the two types of fibre would be kept separate, for use in different types of clothing.

Woollen garments were made, not only for family use but also for export, and many thousands of wool jumpers were sent to Denmark and Norway to clothe their armies. A big part of the Faroese income was derived from the sale of these items, plus knitted socks and stockings, 14,000 pairs of which were exported in 1849! Often, it was the men that did the preparation and spinning of the wool, while the women and children undertook the knitting.

In the beginning, most of the knitted garments were felted, and felted so thickly that it was hard to tell that they had been knitted. The fabric could easily be cut and shaped, and most of the clothing was worn as jackets, trimmed with embroidered facings and laced at the front for the women. Later, the garments were left in their knitted state. As for most of the early Scandinavian pieces, they were knitted in the round to a basic rectangular shape, with bands of small geometric patterns worked in two colours. The colours would alternate in the bands; so, the first band could be of blue bars on a cream background, and the next might be cream chevrons on a blue background. The wool yarn would be fairly coarse and of a similar weight to chunky-weight yarn but knitted on smaller needles to make the resulting fabric more windproof. The women would knit these sweaters while carrying out their normal daily work, sometimes including crossing hills and streams to fetch milk in two pails strapped to their backs!

During the eighteenth century, no one but the Royal Danish Trade Monopoly was allowed to trade in the Faroe Islands, but, in 1856, this was abolished, and it brought about growth in the fishing industry. This in turn led to more demand for warm clothing, as some of the fishing boats would be out at sea for months at a time. The garments that the fishermen favoured were similar to those worn by fishermen all around the Atlantic Ocean and North Sea coasts: plain navy with small seeded patterns of knit and purl stitches.

As happened in Norway in the nineteenth century, the Faroese people also wished to establish a national identity of their own. They have a traditional dress, mostly of black and white, although more colours have since been introduced, and the knitting is very varied. The typical jumper has a plain body and sleeves with a lovely coloured yoke, similar to that of Icelandic knitting, or it has all-over patterns of geometric shapes, as in the pattern here for the trellis sweater.

TRELLIS SWEATER

Size

To fit a chest circumference of 32 (36, 40, 44)in
Actual measurements: chest circumference 36 (38, 42½, 47)in; back length 22 (23, 24, 24½)in; sleeve-seam length 17½in

Materials

7 (7, 8, 9) × 50g balls of Jarol Heritage DK yarn; 55-per-cent wool, 25-per-cent acrylic, 20-per-cent nylon (247m[270yd]/100g) in MC
3 × 50g balls of Jarol Heritage DK yarn; 55-per-cent wool, 25-per-cent acrylic, 20-per-cent nylon (247m[270yd]/100g) in CC

Needles

1 pair 3.25mm needles
1 pair 4mm needles
Circular 3.25mm needle

Tension

21sts and 26 rows to 10cm/4in using 4mm needles over colourwork patt

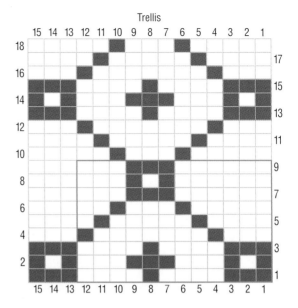

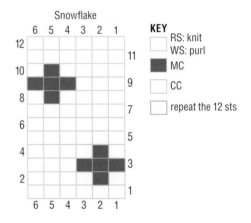

The charts for the trellis sweater.

A close-up of the main colourwork pattern.

Back

Using 3.25mm needles and MC, cast on 87 (99, 111, 123)sts. Work 15 rows of k1, p1 rib.
Change to 4mm needles. Work 10 rows of st. st, and, at the same time, inc evenly to 90 (102, 114, 126)sts on the last row. Work snowflakes chart for 18 (18, 23, 23) rows.

With MC, work 3 rows of st. st, and, at the same time, dec to 87 (99, 111, 123)sts on first row.
Work trellis chart until piece measures 13 (14, 14½, 15)in from cast-on edge.

The all-over pattern of the trellis sweater.

Armhole shaping

Keeping patt correct, cast off 5 (5, 6, 6)sts at beg of next 2 rows.
Dec at each end of alt rows until 71 (75, 79, 85)sts rem.
Work even until armhole measures 8 (8¼, 8½, 9)in.

Shoulder shaping

Cast off 10 (10, 10, 11)sts at beg of next 2 rows and then 10 (11, 11, 12)sts at beg of following 2 rows.
Slip rem 31 (33, 37, 39)sts on to a holder for back neck.

Tip

Cast off the underarm stitches of the front and back by using alternate colours of yarn, to avoid long floats.

Front

Using 3.25mm needles and MC, cast on 87 (99, 111, 123)sts.
Work 15 rows of p1, k1 rib, and, at the same time, inc evenly to 90 (102, 114, 126)sts on the last row.
Change to 4mm needles. Work as for back until armhole measures 5 (5¼, 5½, 6)in, ending with RS facing, having completed a WS row.

Neck shaping

Work 28 (29, 31, 33)sts (for left front), slip next 15 (17, 17, 19)sts on to a holder for front neck, work to end (for right front).
Dec at neck edge of every row 8 (8, 10, 10) times. [20 (21, 21, 23)sts]

Shoulder shaping

Cast off 10 (10, 10, 11)sts at beg of next row and then 10 (11, 11, 12)sts at beg of following alt row.

Return to rem 28 (29, 31, 33)sts for left front, and rejoin yarn with RS facing. Dec at neck edge of every row 8 (8, 10, 10) times. [20 (21, 21, 23)sts]
Cast off 10 (10, 10, 11)sts at beg of next row and then 10 (11, 11, 12)sts at beg of following alt row.

Shoulder seaming

Sew both shoulder seams, to join left front and right front to back.

Sleeves

Using 3.25mm needles, cast on 39 (43, 47, 49)sts.
Work 15 rows of k1, p1 rib, and, at the same time, inc evenly to 41 (47, 51, 51)sts on last row.
Change to 4mm needles. Work as follows, and, at the same time, inc at each end of 5th and then every following 6th row until there are 65 (71, 77, 81)sts:
With MC, work 10 rows of st. st.

A different model wearing the trellis sweater; this colour suits everyone!

A close-up of the small snowflakes pattern that is included at the hem and sleeve edges.

Work snowflakes chart for 18 (18, 23, 23) rows, ensuring that full pattern repeats will be positioned as mirror images on left and right sleeves and taking increase sts into colourwork patt.
With MC, work in st. st.

Sleeve-cap shaping
Cast off 5 (5, 6, 6)sts at beg of next 2 rows. [55 (61, 65, 69)sts]
Dec by 1 stitch at each end of every row until 53 (57, 59, 63)sts rem.

Dec by 1 stitch at each end of alt rows until 23 (27, 31, 33) sts rem.
Dec by 1 stitch at each end of every row until 19 (21, 23, 23)sts rem.
Cast off loosely.

Work second sleeve as for first sleeve, taking into account placement of snowflakes patt.

Neckband

Using a circular 3.25mm needle and MC, knit 31 (33, 37, 39)sts from back-neck holder, pick up and knit 21 (22, 25, 25)sts along left-neck edge, knit 15 (17, 17, 19)sts from front-neck holder and pick up and knit 21 (22, 25, 25)sts along right-neck edge. [88 (94, 104, 108)sts]
Work 8 rounds of k1, p1 rib.
Cast off loosely in patt.

Finishing

Set in sleeves to separate armholes. Sew both side seams and sleeve seams, and weave in all yarn ends.

This jumper could be worked mostly or entirely in the round, either by working the back and front yokes flat or by making steeks at the armholes, followed by picking up stitches of each sleeve around one armhole and working in the round from the sleeve top to the cuff.

FAROES HERITAGE

Knitting is still extremely popular in the Faroe Islands. In April of each year, a knitting festival, *Bindifestivalur*, is held on the islands. There are knitting clubs that meet regularly, just as in many other parts of the world, and the craft seems to be even more popular now than it was in the days when knitting featured as an important part of family incomes.

Many people now think that the famous black-and-white jumper with its band of snowflakes, worn by Sarah Lund in the Danish-inspired US television series *The Killing*, is a Danish design, but it is actually Faroese. It was created by the fashion-design company Gudrun & Gudrun of Tórshavn, run by Gudrun Ludvig and Gudrun Rógvadóttir. They concentrate on sustainability and use the natural products of the Faroe Islands. After experimenting with leather from the local sheep, they turned to specializing in knitting, and all of their garments were originally hand knitted by women on the

islands and now also in projects set up in Jordan and Peru. The two Gudruns derive their inspiration from nature and old stories and from a collection of patterns used on the islands for many years.

Such patterns had eventually been collected and published in *Føroysk Bindingarmynstur* by Hans Debes in 1932, at a time when the Faroe Islands was trying to establish its national identity. Like many collectors before him, he travelled the area, talking to the women who had previously passed on their patterns only by word of mouth, and gathered together as many patterns as he could, collecting over a hundred different motifs for the book in total. Many of the patterns feature geometric blocks of alternate colours, as in the cardigan here, or the type of motifs used in the pattern for the jacket in the collection of the Knitting and Crochet Guild that is shown in Chapter 3.

An all-over pattern similar to one used on the Faroe Islands. This jacket is in the collection of the Knitting and Crochet Guild and was bought from the Folk Industries shop in Bergen.

CHAPTER 6

STITCH DICTIONARY

ARROWHEADS

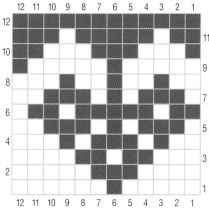

This motif is sometimes inverted and used to represent a row of small trees. It is used across all of the Scandinavian countries and is also seen in Icelandic knitting. It was frequently used on wristlets or above the rib of a cuff.

BINGE

Triangles

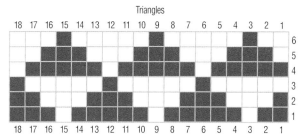

These charts present two very simple Binge patterns that are ideal for using on socks or mittens as well as being alternated on hats. They were frequently knitted in red or blue on a white background.

Dotted diamonds

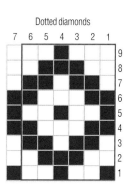

BLOCKS AND DIAMONDS

This is a typical Faroese pattern. Garments featuring this pattern were traditionally knitted in red or blue on a white background, but I followed the idea of hen knitting and worked the featured swatch in gold and burgundy.

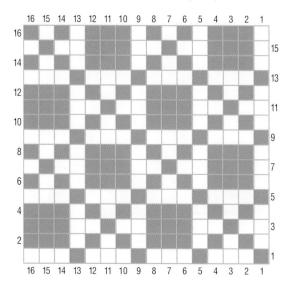

BOHUS

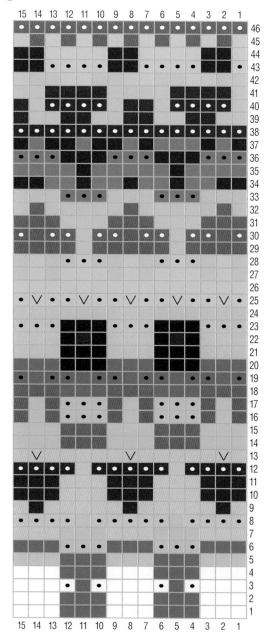

Any of the small patterns in the featured Bohus chart can be combined to make a 'traditional' Bohus-style yoked cardigan or sweater. For example, use rows 9–13 at the beginning, follow this with rows 25–28, work rows 35–41 next and then repeat this sequence but reversing the colours. Some of the Bohus garments were worked in only one colour but with different tones and shades of that colour. The important point to remember is to work some stitches as purl stitches on the right side of the work and to incorporate some 'fluffy'-type yarns.

BORDERS 1 & 2

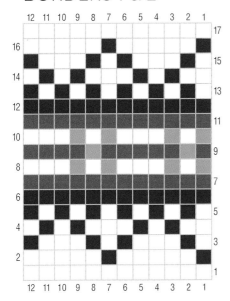

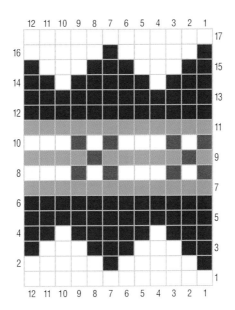

Some of the border patterns used in Scandinavia would often incorporate a third colour in the centre rows. Using more than two colours in a row can be awkward to work and causes the yarns to become tangled, so this approach isn't used now very often.

These small patterns for borders are of the type that would often be used on a long stocking or a double cap. The small plus signs at the bottom were often used on the hems of some garments too. The stylized flowers at the top are also found in Scottish patterns.

CARNATION

There are many variations of the carnation motif. It was often used amongst other motifs of flora and fauna such as those for birds and reindeer. There are also examples of it being worked in colour, especially with a different colour for each row of motifs, and this pattern would be ideal for working with one of the graded-colour yarns.

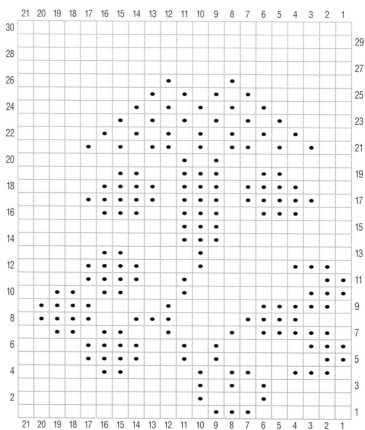

CHEQUERBOARD

This pattern is reminiscent of those used on Sanquhar gloves and would be ideal for a pair of wristlets or mittens. According to James Norbury, it is a pattern from the British Isles, but there is lots of crossover of knitting motifs, and it is also referred to as a Faroe Islands pattern.

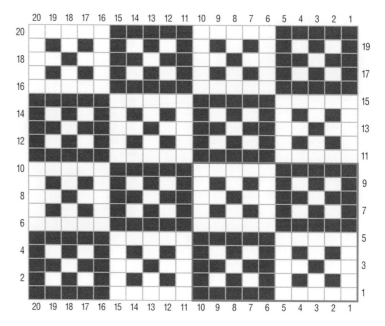

CIRCLE

This is an attractive and versatile geometric motif.

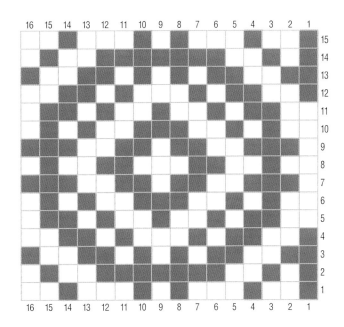

CROSS-AND-DIAMOND BLOCKS

This is another pattern that is also seen in Scotland and possibly derives from the St Andrew's cross.

CROSS AND DIAMONDS

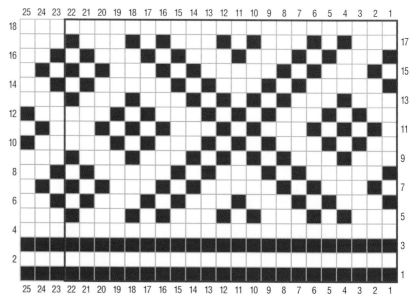

This is a typical design found on sweaters from Setesdal. It could be used around a hat or the top of a stocking.

DANISH STARS

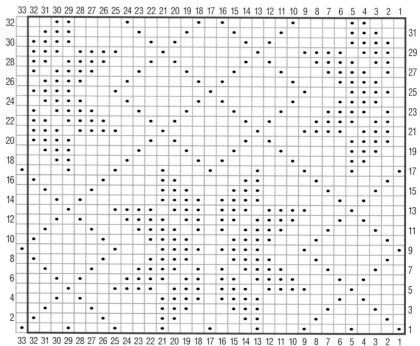

This is a scaled-down version of the pattern found on the fragment of Danish knitting dating from the seventeenth century (see Chapter 5). It was a widely used pattern and has also been seen on silk jackets and in coloured versions in Sweden and the Faroe Islands, respectively.

DIAMOND BORDER

This is a small pattern that is useful for hats and stockings but also as a border above hems and cuffs. To make it larger, work another diamond outside and around it, and turn the single dots into plus signs or crosses.

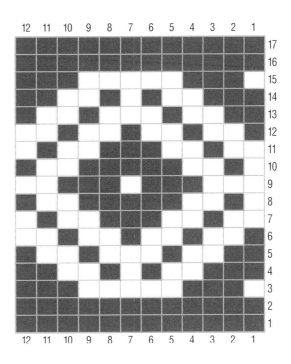

ENCLOSED STAR

This is another of the ubiquitous textured-star motifs. These would sometimes appear as an enlarged version on the body of the garment and as small versions on the sleeves.

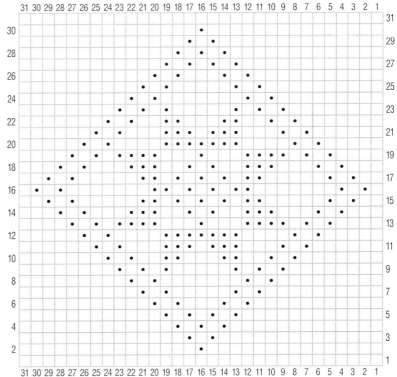

FIR TREE

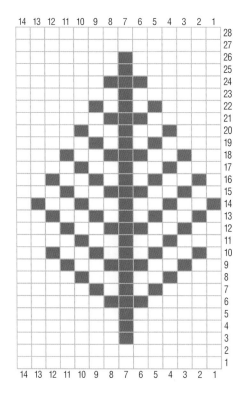

This is a popular design throughout the world. It was seen as a sign of long life and is referred to as the 'Tree of Life' in many cultures. The same design can be worked as textured stitches, and, as such, it was frequently used on fishermen's jerseys as a link back to the land.

FLOWERS IN DIAMONDS

This is another design that can also be worked as textured stitches and which was used in that way on the nattrojer. The coloured version is another Faroese pattern.

HEARTS BORDER

This is a more modern design seen in Fair Isle as well as Scandinavian knitting. It would make an attractive cuff for a pair of mittens.

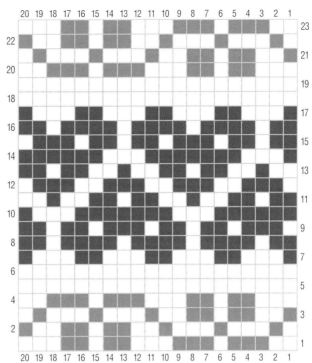

LARGE CROSS

This is a slightly larger version of the cross-and-diamonds pattern used in Setesdal.

LARGE SNOWFLAKE

This is the same design as used in many Fair Isle patterns but worked with a single contrast colour. It is said that the curled sections were inspired by ram's horns.

LARGE SNOWFLAKE WITH FERNS

The ubiquitous eight-pointed star has been rounded off here and as such is more frequently used in Sweden. The more straight-sided version is the Norwegian one.

LUSEKOFTE

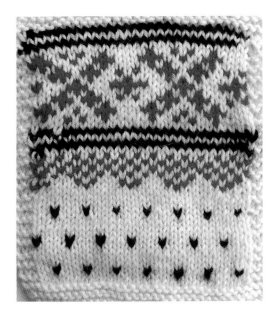

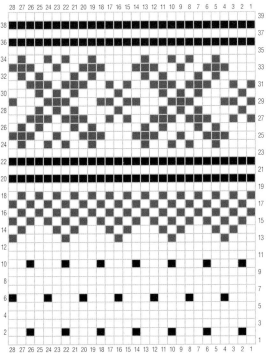

This is another typical pattern from the Setesdal region of Norway.

MITTEN FILL-INS 1 & 2

These mitten fill-in-1 and mitten fill-in-2 motifs would be ideal for use on mittens as an alternative to the Selbu rose. Add a few small cross or diamond shapes to fill in the gaps around these prominent motifs. The mitten fill-in-1 pink diamond would fit nicely into the pointed top of a mitten.

MITTEN PALMS 1 & 2

There are various ways of decorating the palms of mittens, including the three patterns presented here. The palm patterns are often of less elaborate designs than those of the upper hands.

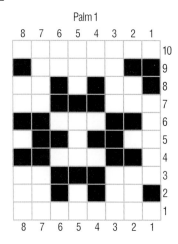

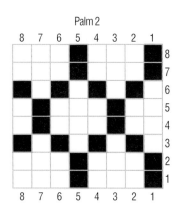

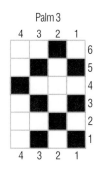

OWL

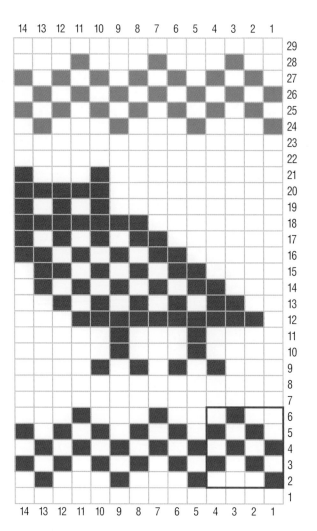

Motifs of flora and fauna were often used in Scandinavian designs. This little owl could be incorporated into a design for a pair of mittens or be placed along the hem of a sweater. Like the reindeer motif that follows, it could also be worked as a textured motif.

REINDEER

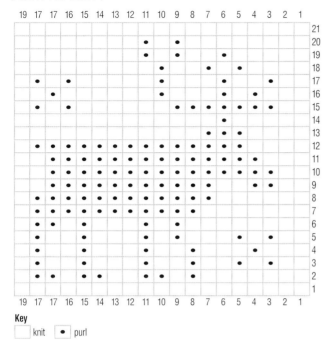

Key

| | knit | • | purl |

This could be worked as a textured motif or be knitted in two colours. Use it around the hem of a hat or cuffs of a pair of mittens. The written instructions for this design to be worked in the round are as follows:

Round 1: Knit. (19sts)
Round 2: K7, p1, k1, p2, k2, (p2, k1) × 2.
Round 3: K2, p1, k1, (p1, k2) × 2, p1, k3, p1, k2, p1, k1.
Round 4: K3, (p1, k3, p1, k2) × 2, p1, k1.
Round 5: K2, (p1, k1, p1, k3) × 2, p1, k2, p1, k1.
Round 6: K8, p1, k1, p1, k3, p1, k1, p2, k1.
Round 7: K7, p11, k1.
Round 8: K6, p12, k1.
Round 9: K2, p2, k2, p11, k2.
Round 10: K2, p15, k2.
Round 11: K3, p14, k2.
Round 12: K4, p14, k1.
Round 13: K4, p3, k12.
Round 14: K5, p1, k13.
Round 15: K2, p7, k6, (p1, k1) × 2.
Round 16: K3, p1, k1, p1, k3, p1, k6, p1, k2.
Round 17: (K2, p1) × 2, k3, p1, k5, (p1, k1) × 2.
Round 18: K4, p1, k1, p1, k2, p1, k9.
Round 19: K5, p1, k2, p1, k1, p1, k8.
Round 20: K8, p1, k1, p1, k8.
Round 21: Knit.

ROUNDED SNOWFLAKE

This is a less elaborate version of the typical rounded-snowflake motif and again, probably derived from a Fair Isle motif.

SMALL DAMASK STAR

This little star was widely used in Denmark and the Faroe Islands, often on the sleeves of a garment with a plain-knitted, or sometimes a fabric, body.

The written instructions for this design to be worked in the round are as follows:

Rounds 1–2: Knit. (14sts)
Round 3: K4, p1, k5, p1, k3.
Round 4: K4, (p2, k3) × 2.
Round 5: K4, p3, k1, p3, k3.
Round 6: K5, p5, k4.
Round 7: K2, (p3, k1) × 3.
Round 8: K3, p3, k1, p1, k1 p3, k2.
Round 9: Rep round 5.
Round 10: Rep round 8.
Round 11: Rep round 7.
Round 12: Rep round 6.
Round 13: Rep round 5.
Round 14: Rep round 4.
Round 15: Rep round 3.
Rounds 16–17: Knit.

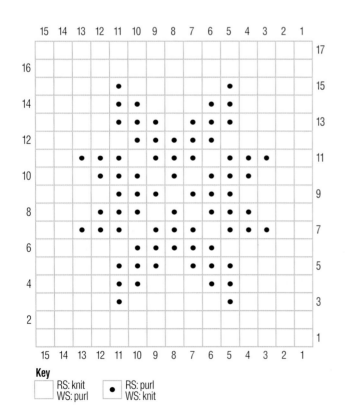

Key

| | RS: knit WS: purl | | • | RS: purl WS: knit |

SMALL DIVIDERS

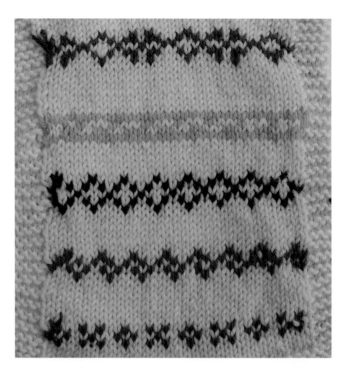

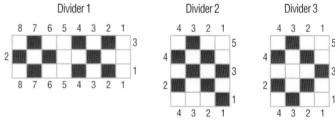

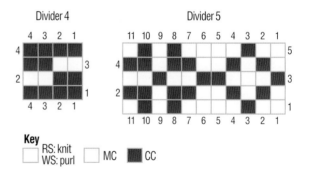

Key

| | RS: knit WS: purl | | | MC | | CC |

These patterns are used between large motifs in a similar way to peeries on a Fair Isle garment. Some of them could also be used on the palms and thumbs of mittens.

SMALL STAR

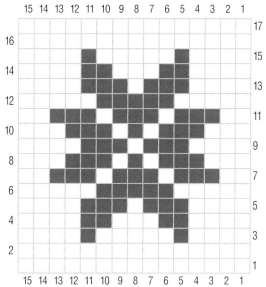

This is the same design as the small damask star but worked in colour, usually as a row of stars.

STAR WITH DIAMONDS

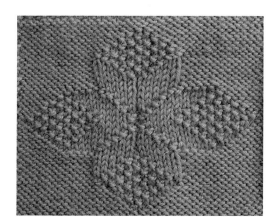

This is a variation of a damask-star pattern.

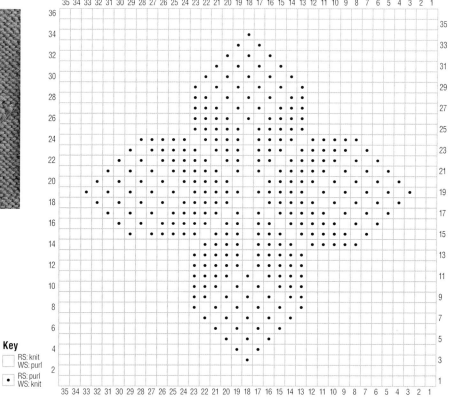

Key

▢ RS: knit
WS: purl

▪ RS: purl
WS: knit

STAR WITH SMALL DIAMONDS

This is a further variation of a damask-star pattern.

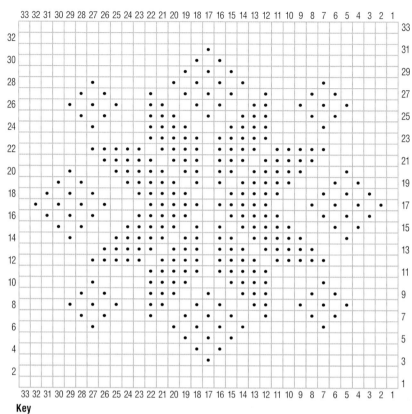

TRAILING LEAVES

This was the most frequently used motif to be included around the cuffs of mittens.

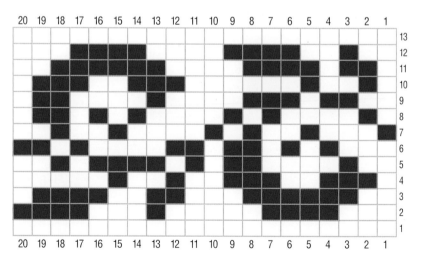

TWINED-3 STITCH

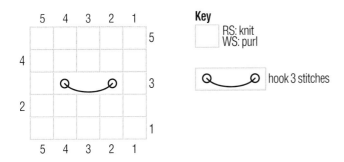

This stitch is also known as a crook stitch or hook stitch and is worked with two strands of yarn. It is achieved by working the sequence of k1 with first strand, bring second strand to front, p1 with second strand, leave second strand at front, k1 with first strand, p1 with second strand, take second strand to back, k1 with first strand.

TWINED-5 STITCH

This stitch is a wider version of the twined-3 stitch. It is again known as a crook stitch or hooked stitch and is worked with two strands of yarn. It is achieved by working the sequence of k1 with first strand, bring second strand to front, p1 with second strand, leave second strand at front, k1 with first strand, p1 with second strand, leave second strand at front, k1 with first strand, p1 with second strand, take second strand to back, k1 with first strand.

TWINED DIAMOND

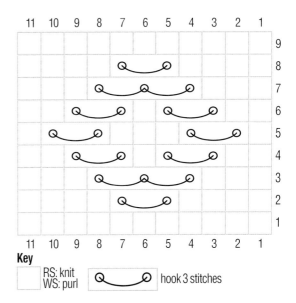

The written instructions for this design to be worked in the round are as follows:

Round 1: Knit. (11sts)
Round 2: K4, work a twined-3 st, k4.
Round 3: K3, work a twined-5 st (see the accompanying section 'Twined-5 stitch'), k3.
Round 4: K2, work a twined-3 st, k1, work twined-3 st, k2.
Round 5: K1, work a twined-3 st, k3, work twined-3 st, k1.
Round 6: Rep round 4.
Round 7: Rep round 3.
Round 8: Rep round 2.
Round 9: Knit.

YOKE 1

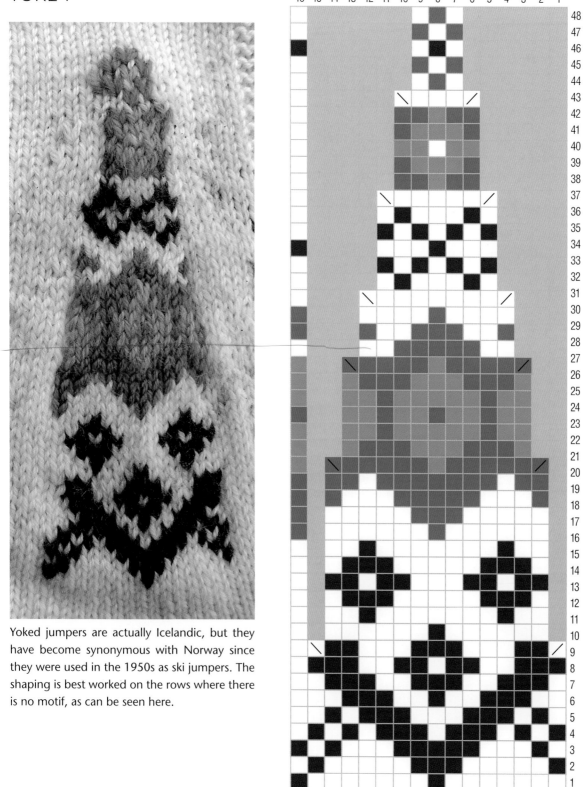

Yoked jumpers are actually Icelandic, but they have become synonymous with Norway since they were used in the 1950s as ski jumpers. The shaping is best worked on the rows where there is no motif, as can be seen here.

Key

⟋ k2tog

⟍ ssk

YOKE 2

Here is another suggestion for working a colourwork yoke. It could be worked from the top down, by working increases where the stitches are marked as decreases on the chart.

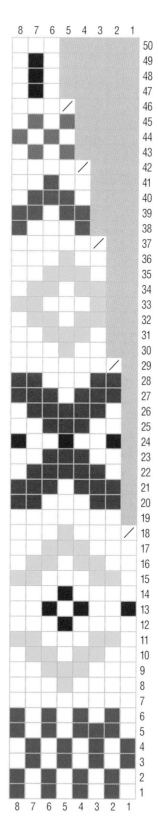

Key

 k2tog

CHAPTER 7

GENERIC PATTERNS

To help you to make good use of the stitch dictionary in Chapter 6, I have included some generic styles with schematics here so that you can add your own motifs to them. Try to centralize the main motif by working out the placement on squared paper, starting with the central stitch of the motif and working outwards. For the motifs in Chapter 6, the number of stitches required for each motif is stated, but note that some of the motifs have main-colour (background-colour) squares (or sometimes empty squares) at the sides. Don't count these in your motif stitch count, as you may want to add more than one stitch between them. When working out how many motifs will fit across a piece of knitting, remember that there will be one more space than there are motifs, just as there are for buttonholes. Use the schematic shapes to make schematics of your own, and mark your measurements and/or stitch counts on them.

Many of the traditional Scandinavian sweaters would be knitted as four rectangles: the back, the front and two sleeves, which were sometimes knitted downward from the armhole but more often knitted from the cuff upwards. I have mainly written the garment patterns in this book as though the sleeves were knitted cuff upwards, but it is an easy matter to work them the other way up, by picking up the correct number of stitches around the armholes. This usually entails picking up 3 stitches for every 4 rows of the body, and, if you do this to begin with, you can always increase or decrease stitches evenly in the next round as necessary.

Most of the schematics featured here have been developed and calculated based on the garment being worked with a DK-weight yarn to produce a fabric with a tension of 22sts and 28 rows to 10cm/4in, using whichever needles gives you that tension. The numbers on the schematics are for the stitches and rows at that tension, not the measurements, for a particular dimension of the garment. Copy the shapes of the schematics, and add your own measurements with the tension that you get for your chosen yarn and needles. And remember to add in the amount of ease that you want too. At a tension of 22sts to 4in, the garment represented by the first schematic will actually measure almost 44in around the widest part of the chest (corresponding to the 120sts for the front and for the back as listed on the schematic). This measurement is based on there being 5½sts to 1in (that is, one quarter of 22sts); therefore, 120sts divided by 5½ equals a width of exactly 21.8in for the front and the same for the back. This means that the garment measures exactly 43.6in in circumference once the front and the back are joined together.

PERCENTAGE METHOD

Before the publication of printed patterns for knitting, the knitters of the past each worked out for themselves how many stitches and rows they needed to work for a particular person's sweater. They did this by calculating the relevant numbers by using percentages for the various parts of the body. If you want to base your design on the shapes given here but your swatch has an entirely different tension, work out the number of stitches for the various sections based on the percentage method.

Begin by calculating how many stitches you need for the chest width, plus whatever extra you want to add for ease. In the example given first, this number is 120 stitches. Supposing you have 20 stitches to 4in, which is 5 stitches to 1in, and you want the finished garment to measure 21in across the widest part. Multiply 21 by 5, which gives you 105 stitches, or 210 stitches if you are working in the round.

For an adult, the neck circumference needs to be approximately 40 per cent of the complete circumference of the garment. For 210 stitches, 40 per cent is 84 stitches, so leave 42 stitches for the back neck and one third of this number (which equals 14) for the straight part of the centre-front neck. Leave those stitches on a holder as you work the left and the right parts separately, gradually shaping each part by decreasing on every row for about 1in and continuing to work decreases at the neck edge on alternate rows over the rest of the stitches until you have decreased by 14 stitches.

The wrist is about 20 per cent of the complete circumference of the garment; 20 per cent of 210 stitches is 42 stitches. The upper arm is about 50 per cent of the complete circumference; 50 per cent of 210 stitches is 105 stitches (104 or 106 stitches, rounded to the nearest even number). When you know the required length of your sleeve and how many rows you get to the inch, you can calculate how frequently to work pairs of increases, to increase from 42 stitches to 104 stitches.

These numbers work for a square, drop-shouldered sweater or for a yoked sweater, for which there is the added step of calculating for the shaping of the yoke. When you know the required depth of the yoke from the neck edge to the underarm and you know the number of rows you have per inch, work out how to gradually decrease from the total number of stitches of the body and two sleeves to the 84 stitches that you need for the neck opening.

The schematics here are based on the proportions of the average person. You might want to alter the number of rows of a garment for someone who is tall or for someone who is short, but, as always, the best fit comes from taking accurate measurements, and the percentage system is only a guide.

ROUND-NECK, SET-IN-SLEEVE SWEATER WITH HOOD

The first schematic is for a sweater with a round neck, set-in sleeves and a hood. However, you could omit the hood and work a basic ribbed band if you prefer. If you do choose to add the hood, work it in the same pattern as the body of the sweater.

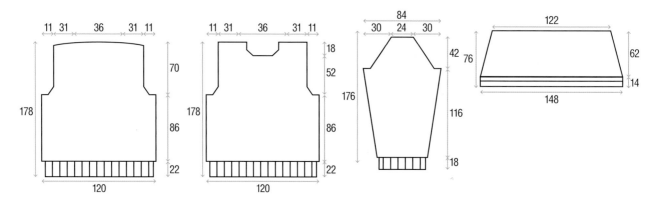

A hooded-sweater schematic.

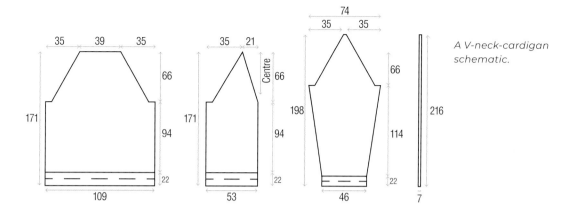

A V-neck-cardigan schematic.

RAGLAN CARDIGAN WITH V-NECK

The second schematic is for a V-neck cardigan with raglan sleeves. It would fit a person with a 36in chest comfortably and would measure just under 40in in circumference. In this example the stitches for the two fronts are increased to 56 on the last row of the rib.

ROUND-NECK, SET-IN-SLEEVE SWEATER

This schematic is for a round-neck, set-in-sleeve, hip-length sweater; this is a slightly larger garment, with an actual chest measurement of about 50in. It is a unisex style and could easily be adapted into a jacket by making it longer and splitting the front in two. Patch or side-seam pockets would make the garment useful for outdoor wear.

TRADITIONAL SQUARE-SHAPED SWEATER WORKED WITH ARAN-WEIGHT WOOL

The next schematic is one of a traditional square-shaped sweater to be worked in a thicker, aran-weight wool, giving 18 stitches and 24 rows to 10cm/4in. The sweater would be ideal for featuring a band of Norwegian stars. This size could accommodate six of the large snowflake-with-ferns motifs with 3 stitches between each or five of the large-snowflake motifs with 2 stitches between each. Quite often, the number of motifs that will fit into a design does not work exactly for all sizes. In this case, you either alter the number of stitches between the motifs, add an extra small motif, or, if the mis-match is out by only a small number of stitches, decrease or increase by the number of stitches required on the first plain round before starting to work the motif. Remember to either increase or decrease back to the original stitch number after the pattern panel is finished or take the change in stitch

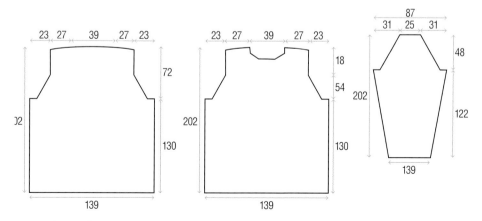

A round-neck-sweater schematic.

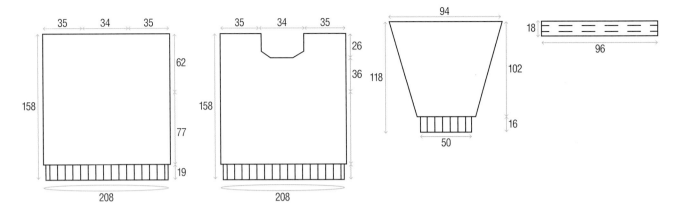

A roll-neck-sweater schematic.

number into account when shaping the neck. For a cardigan or jacket, you would quite likely have only half a motif at the front edges, so choose to use a motif or pattern that will still look attractive when it is divided in this manner.

This is a basic drop-shouldered sweater that will fit a person with up to a 46in chest circumference, and it could be knitted flat or in the round. This example has a roll neck, but it could be adapted to have a polo neck by working more rows.

If you are working this garment shape in the round, for a slightly more comfortable fit, you can insert a gusset under the arms. Mark the position of the side 'seams' with a purl stitch. Approximately 4in below the start of the armhole, increase by 1 stitch on each side of this purl stitch, and work those increases as purl stitches but with the centre 'seam' stitch from now on being worked as a knit stitch. After 3 rows, increase again on each side of the knit stitch as before. Work the stitches adjacent to the new increase stitches as knit stitches. Continue to increase on every 4th row as established until your gusset is about 3in wide. When you reach the position of the armholes, leave these stitches on a holder and either work the back and the front separately or add a few stitches as steeks in the gaps between the front and the back and continue working in the round until the body is finished. The gusset stitches are incorporated into the sleeve and gradually decreased until there is one stitch left, which becomes the false seam of the sleeve.

The sleeves for this garment could be knitted by first joining the shoulders of the back and the front, marking the row edge where the armhole begins, then picking up 94 stitches around the armhole between those markers. Work each sleeve downwards, gradually decreasing to the 50 stitches of the cuff. Alternatively, the sleeves can be worked cuff upwards and then joined to the body either by sewing them in or

leaving the stitches live at the top of the sleeve and joining them by grafting or with a three-needle cast-off. For the latter method, pick up and knit 94 stitches around the armhole first, then cast them off together with the corresponding stitches of the top of the sleeve. An old method of joining a sleeve to the garment body was by passing each live stitch at the top of the sleeve through the adjacent edge stitch of the armhole and then casting off the live stitches as they are passed through, by passing the previously passed-through stitch over the just-passed-through stitch, as when casting off.

MITTENS

Here is the generic mitten template for a medium-sized adult hand. Print it out twice, and fill in different patterns for the upper hand and the palm. Note that this template is presented for the palm of the left hand, but it can be easily adapted for the palm of the right hand by mirroring the position of the stitches to be knitted with waste yarn, for the afterthought thumb. By omitting the stitches to be knitted with waste yarn, the template can be used for the right and left upper hands.

To work the mitten thumb, pick up 20 stitches where waste yarn was used to mark the placement of the thumb and provide a means of later accessing live stitches to work the thumb. Work even for about 2½in and then decrease to 8 stitches. Leaving a tail, cut the yarn, thread it through the live stitches, draw up the stitches, to close the hole at the top of the thumb, and fasten off.

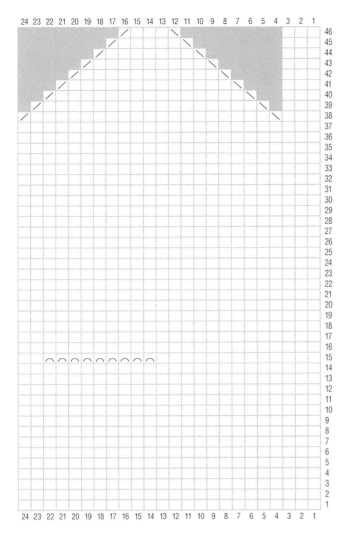

A blank chart for the designing of a colourwork mitten.

YOKED JUMPER

For what you might call a 'typical Norwegian jumper', this is a general pattern with a round yoke. When you have joined the pieces for working of the yoke, you will have 240 (256, 272, 288) stitches. All of the numbers are divisible by 8, and the first and last sizes will accommodate a 24-stitch repeat, so one of the larger patterns would work for these two sizes. If none of your preferred charts will fit the size you require, consider adapting the charts by adding filler stitches between them, as I have done for the hot-water-bottle cover.

You could also use this pattern for a Bohus-style jumper, as most of the motifs of this style are multiples of 4 stitches or are small enough for it not to matter if they don't fit exactly around the relevant body circumference.

Size

Small (medium, large, XL)
Actual measurements: chest circumference 35 (38½, 42, 45)in; back length (bottom hem to underarm) 15 (15½, 16½, 17)in; sleeve length 17 (17½, 18, 18½)in

Materials

450 (500, 550, 600)g (approx) of aran-weight yarn

Needles

Circular 4.5mm needle
Circular 5mm needle

Tension

18sts and 24 rows to 10cm/4in using 5mm needles over st. st

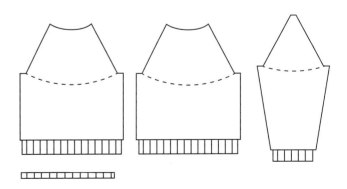

A yoked-jumper schematic.

A yoked jumper from Norway. Item NF 2012-0771 Anne-Lise Reinsfelt/Norsk Folkemuseum.

Body

Worked in the round.

Using a circular 4.5mm needle and MC, cast on 160 (176, 192, 208)sts, and join to work in the round. Work 2 (2, 2½, 2½)in of k1, p1 rib.

Change to a circular 5mm needle, and work your chosen chart for colourwork border above hem.

Cont in st. st with MC until work measures 15 (15½, 16½, 17)in from cast-on edge.

Slip all sts on to holder.

Sleeves

Worked in the round.

Using 4.5mm needles and MC, cast on 40 (42, 44, 46)sts, and join to work in the round. Work 2in of k1, p1 rib. Change to 5mm needles.

Next round: Cont in st. st, and, at the same time, inc evenly by 0 (2, 0, 2)sts across round. [40 (44, 44, 48)sts]

Work a border if required, then:

Cont in st. st, and, at the same time, inc at beg and end of every 8th round until there are 60 (64, 68, 72)sts.

Work even in st. st until piece measures 17 (17½, 18, 18½)in from cast-on edge.

Slip last 5 (6, 7, 8)sts of round and first 5 (6, 7, 8)sts of round on to holder for underarm.

Work second sleeve as for first sleeve.

Joining body and sleeves

Join body and sleeves as follows:

Place last 5 (6, 7, 8)sts and first 5 (6, 7, 8)sts of body on to holder for left underarm.

Using a circular 5mm needle and MC, knit across 50 (52, 54, 56) sts of left sleeve, k70 (76, 82, 88)sts for front, place next 10 (12, 14, 16)sts of body on to holder for right underarm, knit across 50 (52, 54, 56) sts of right sleeve and then k70 (76, 82, 88)sts for back. [240 (256, 272, 288)sts]

Work 1 round or 2 rounds with MC.

Yoke

Work from your chosen chart(s), and dec where indicated to shape the yoke until chart is completed and there are 90 (96, 102, 108)sts.

Work 1 round with MC.

Neckband

Using a circular 4.5mm needle and MC, dec to 70 (72, 74, 76)sts as follows:

Small: K5, (k2, k2tog) to last 5sts, k5.
Med: (K2, k2tog) to end.
Large: K9, (k1, k2tog) to last 9sts, k9.
XL: K6, (k1, k2tog) to last 6sts, k6.

Work 9 rows of k1, p1 rib.

Cast off loosely in patt.

Finishing

Graft or cast-off each set of sleeve and body stitches for each underarm. Weave in all yarn ends.

Jumpers like this one are often worked from the top down nowadays. If you wanted to work in this way then cast on 70 (72, 74, 76)sts and work a ribbed neckband, then follow the provided instructions but increase where it says to decrease throughout and cast on the appropriate number of stitches for the underarms. Work the body stitches in the round, finishing with the rib hem, then work each sleeve separately in the round.

SLOUCHY HAT

Here is a pattern for a generic slouchy hat. This one could be worked with the Bjarbo pattern or any of the other patterns that have a repeat that will fit into 120 stitches.

Size

To fit an average adult head of about 20in in circumference

Materials

100g of any DK-weight yarn in MC
50g of any DK-weight yarn in CC1
50g of any DK-weight yarn in CC2

Needles

5 double-pointed 3.25mm needles (or an equivalent circular needle, if preferred)

5 double-pointed 4mm needles (or an equivalent circular needle, if preferred)

Tension

22sts and 28 rows to 10cm/4in using 4mm needles over st. st

Key

■ MC □ CC1 ■ CC2 □ repeat

The Bjarbo chart for the slouchy hat. (A swatch worked from this chart is shown in Chapter 4.)

Using 3.25mm needles and CC1, cast on 108sts, and join to work in the round. Work 2 rounds of k2, p2 rib.
Change to MC, and cont in rib for 2in.
Next round: Inc as follows: (k8, m1, k1) × 12. (120sts)
Change to 4mm needles, and work your chosen border chart, work 1 round with MC and then work pattern repeat for rounds 1–34 of Bjarbo chart.
Cont with MC until work measures length required for hat depth, then work crown shaping as follows:
Round 1: (K10, k2tog) to end.
Round 2 and every alt, even-numbered round: Knit, following a small border chart or working round with CC1 or CC2, if desired.
Round 3: (K9, k2tog) to end.
Round 5: (K8, k2tog) to end.
Round 7: (K7, k2tog) to end.
Round 9: (K6, k2tog) to end.
Round 11: (K5, k2tog) to end.
Round 13: (K4, k2tog) to end.
Round 15: (K3, k2tog) to end.
Round 17: (K2, k2tog) to end.

Round 19: (K1, k2tog) to end.
Round 21: K2tog to end.
Leaving a tail, cut yarn, thread yarn through rem sts, draw up sts, to close the hole at the top of the hat, and fasten off. Weave in all yarn ends.

Finishing

Wet the hat, gently squeeze out the water and then fit the hat over an appropriately sized basin, plate or balloon, and leave the fabric to dry naturally.

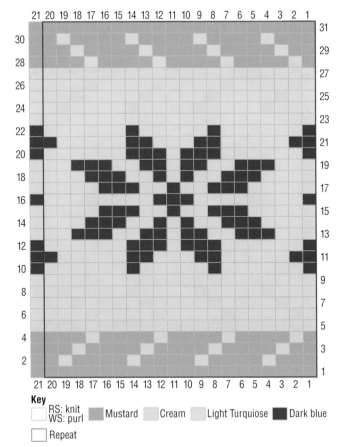

Key
RS: knit WS: purl	(white)
Mustard	
Cream	
Light Turquiose	
Dark blue	
Repeat	

The snowflake scarf chart.

SNOWFLAKE SCARF

Size

Length 52in; width 6½in

Materials

200g Main colour (MC) DK
Oddments of three other colours

Needles

1 pair 4mm needles

Using MC, cast on 41sts and work 5in st st ending with a RS row. Knit one row on WS to mark foldline.
Now work from chart for 5in.
Increase to 45sts evenly across the row and work in rib for 42in.
Decrease to 41sts evenly across the row then work from chart again.
Knit 1 row on WS to mark foldline then cont in st st for 5in.
Cast off.

Fold st st portions of MC to wrong side and stitch in place, leaving one side open if you would like to use these as 'pockets'.

Make 4 tassels by winding all the contrast colours around your hand or a small book. Thread 2 or 3 strands through the ring and tie them tightly in place. Cut through the strands at the opposite end to this knot. About 1in from the knot, wrap a single strand tightly around the tassel and tie it firmly. Thread it back through the top of the tassel and use it to attach the tassel to the scarf.

Alternatively, you could make some knitted curls. Cast on a number of stitches depending on how long you want the curls to be. Knit a row increasing in every stitch. Knit 1 more row. Cast off loosely.

Attach one tassel to each corner of the scarf or a row of curls along the short edges.

The snowflake scarf.

NECK COSY

Size
One size

Materials
2 X 50g balls 4ply in main colour (MC)
1 x 50 g ball in each of 3 contrasting colours

Needles
1 circular 2.75mm needle
1 circular 3.25mm needle

Begin at neck edge. Cast on 108sts using size 2.75mm needle. Join into a ring, being careful not to twist.
Work 5 ins K1 P1 rib.
Change to 3.25mm needle and knit 1 round then working in st st, follow chart, making invisible increases by working into the right or left leg of the stitch where indicated.
When chart is completed, work 1 round in main colour then 8 rounds K1 P1 rib.
Cast off loosely.

The neck cosy.

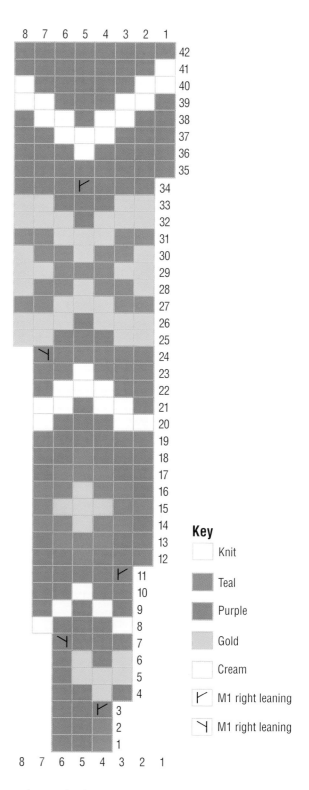

The neck cosy chart.

Key
☐	Knit
■	Teal
■	Purple
■	Gold
☐	Cream
⊢	M1 right leaning
⊣	M1 right leaning

LEGWARMERS

Size

Around widest part of leg 14in

Length of leg 12in; adjustable

Materials

100gms of each of 4 colours of DK (I used Blacker Swan)

Needles

3.5mm and 4mm needles (dpns or circular)

Tension

22sts and 28 rounds to 4in over rib on 4.5mm needles

The leg warmers.

These can be knitted in the round or flat. If they are knitted in the round, repeat the chart within the red border, placing a marker at the beginning of the round. When knitting flat, cast on an extra stitch, repeat the chart within the border to the last stitch and knit the stitch outside the border.

Work two the same.

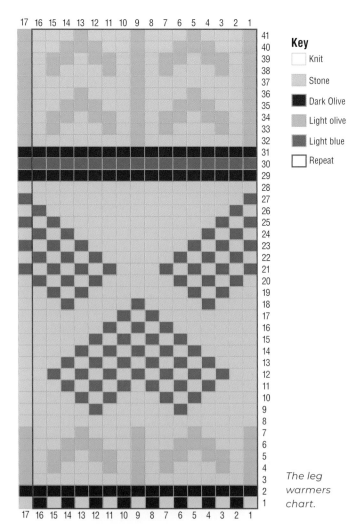

Key

- ☐ Knit
- ☐ Stone
- ■ Dark Olive
- ☐ Light olive
- ☐ Light blue
- ☐ Repeat

The leg warmers chart.

Begin at the top of the leg.

Using 4mm needles and casting on using the thumb method, make a slip knot with about 36in of blue and about 4in of stone. With the blue around the thumb, cast on 64 sts (not including the slip knot, which you now remove). Break off the blue.

Change to 3.5mm needles and work 1½in K1 P1 rib in Stone.

Change to 4mm needles and continue in st st following chart. When chart is finished, continue in main colour until leg is desired length, decreasing 1 st at beg and end of row/round on next and every 6th row/round to 58 sts.

Using dark green, work as row 2 of chart then work 1 row/round in dark green. Break off dark green and continue in stone, knit 1 row.

Change to 3.5mm needles and work 1 in K1 P1 rib.

Cast off loosely.

BIBLIOGRAPHY

Bohn, A.S. *Norwegian Knitting Designs* (Spinningwheel, 2011), ISBN-13: 9780979312618

Høxbro, V. *Knit to be Square: Domino designs to knit and felt* (Interweave Press, 2008), ISBN-13: 9781596680890

Keele, W. *Poems of Color: Knitting in the Bohus tradition* (Interweave Press, 1995), ISBN-13: 9781883010126

Lavold, E. *Viking Patterns for Knitting: Inspiration and projects for today's knitter* (Trafalgar Square Books, 2015), ISBN-13: 9781570767265

Mathiassen, T.E., Nosch, M.-L., Ringgaard, M., Toftegaard, K., Pederson, M.V. *Fashionable Encounters: Perspectives and trends in textile and dress in the Early Modern Nordic World* (Oxbow Books, 2014), ISBN-13: 9781782973829

Rutt, R. *A History of Hand Knitting* (Batsford, 1989), ISBN-13: 9780713451184

INDEX

RELATED TITLES FROM CROWOOD

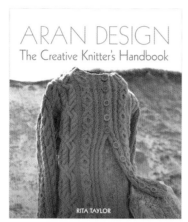

978 1 78500 407 0

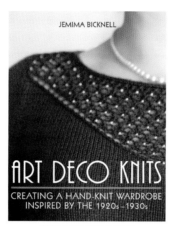

978 1 78500 549 7

978 1 78500 697 5

978 1 78500 455 1

978 1 78500 029 4

978 1 78500 507 7

9 781 78500 571 8

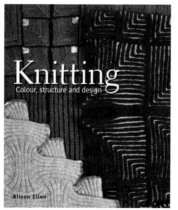

978 1 84797 284 2

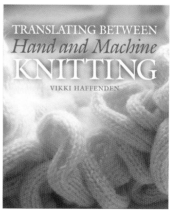

978 1 78500 431 5